Funding in action:

Reportage on the EU's Instrument for Stability

The contents of this publication do not necessarily reflect the opinion or position of the European Commission's Directorate-General for External Relations.

For weekly news by e-mail from the Directorate-General for External Relations, please visit this site: http://ec.europa.eu/comm/external_relations/feedback/weekly.htm

Editor - Andrea Ricci
Project Manager - Olaf Deussen
Editorial Manager - Jernett Karensen
Art Director - Gregorie Desmons
Project Assistant - Bram Blondeel

Europe Direct is a service to help you find answers to your questions about the European Union

Freephone number (*):
00 800 6 7 8 9 10 11

(*)Certain mobile telephone operators do not allow access to 00 800 numbers or these calls may be billed.

A great deal of additional information on the European Union is available on the Internet. It can be accessed through the Europa server (http://europa.eu).

Cataloguing data can be found at the end of this publication.

Luxembourg: Office for Official Publications of the European Communities, 2008

ISBN 978-92-79-07033-4

Printed in Belgium

PRINTED ON WHITE CHLORINE-FREE PAPER

ACKNOWLEDGEMENTS

The European Commission's Directorate-General for External Relations and the editor of this book Andrea Ricci wish to thank all those without whom this work would not have been possible: first and foremost all the authors (writers and photojournalists) who contributed to making this report special, then all the people involved in turning warnings into action; Christian Berger (Head of the Crisis Response and Peacebuilding Unit of DG RELEX) and our colleagues in the geographic units and those working in the EC Delegations on the ground. Finally a big thank you to all those men and women in various NGOs and international organisations who have teamed up with the European Commission in implementing the first wave of IfS projects.

Thanks to the devoted team from GOPA-Cartermill for their patient and tireless work conceiving this book; Olaf Deussen (Project Manager), Jernett Karensen and Adrian Veale (Editorial Managers), Gregorie Desmons (Art Director), Telm Borras (Production Manager), Bram Blondeel (Project Assistant) and the journalists: Cillian Donnelly, Gareth Harding, Chris Coakley, Patricia McCracken, Daniela Schröder, Juliane von Reppert-Bismarck, Maria-Laura Franciosi and Amy Shifflette.

Finally warm thanks to Martine Robin and Anne-Lyse Tardivat of Agence VU, Nick Pappadopoulos of Agence VII, Etienne Miesen of AFP, Laurent Dumont of AP and Chi-Keat Man of the Telegraph Media Group who all played a critical role in keeping us connected with the photojournalists.

FOREWORD

Over the last two years the European Union has made major steps forward in how to deal with international crises and natural disasters.

First, financial resources for crisis response interventions have grown substantially, reaching into the budget for CFSP/ESDP operations and the new Instrument for Stability. The year 2008 began with major EU operations in Chad and Kosovo as well as 20 ongoing and planned crisis response projects under the Stability Instrument, around the world. In addition, European institutions have strengthened their operational cooperation.

Secondly, progress is being made in the integration of EU resources with those of European Union member states, NGOs and the think tank community in Europe and beyond. We are developing a new 'Peace-building Partnership' to promote closer co-operation between NGOs, EU institutions and Member States.

Thirdly, we have been focusing on how to mobilise our efforts to act faster on the basis of reliable early warning information, a key challenge for the European Union in the field of crisis response and peace-building.

Progress in all three areas is geared towards more effective action. This reportage shows examples of this action underway within projects launched under the EU's Instrument for Stability. It features insights from partners involved in the projects on the ground, and from European Commission officials overseeing the Instrument and the way it can provide the best response to crisis and disaster.

Much remains to be done, but I believe that these projects show ways in which peace can be – and is being – built.

Benita Ferrero-Waldner

Introduction
The Instrument for Stability

Regulation
EC 1717/2006, in force since 1 January 2007

Budget
2007-2013: €2,062 million

- Crisis response and preparedness: €1,587 million

- Non-proliferation of WMD: €266 million

- Trans-regional security threats: €118 million

- Administrative expenditure: €91 million

Objectives

(1) to ensure an effective, rapid, flexible and adequately funded initial response to situations of political crisis or natural disaster in third countries;

(2) to develop, longer-term Community actions to counter global and trans-regional threats arising from organised crime, trafficking, proliferation of nuclear, biological and chemical agents and also threats to critical infrastructure and public health;

(3) to set up longer-term capacity building measures aimed at strengthening international organisations and non-state actors with a crisis prevention or response mandate.

Implemented through:

- Strategy Paper 2007-2011
- Indicative Programme 2007-2008 } long-term measures
- Annual Work Programmes
- Crisis response projects (short-term) for 2008
- Peace-building Partnership launched November 2007

FROM THE RAPID REACTION MECHANISM TO THE INSTRUMENT FOR STABILITY

In 2001 the European Commission launched the Rapid Reaction Mechanism (RRM) with the intention of allowing the EC to respond quickly and effectively to conflict and crisis situations around the globe.

The RRM was managed and coordinated through the Conflict Prevention and Crisis Management Unit in the European Commission's External Relations Directorate-General (DG RELEX).

The RRM has been used in many countries, including FYROM (Former Yugoslav Republic of Macedonia), Indonesia (Papua), Ivory Coast, Liberia, Sri Lanka, Bolivia, Vietnam, Burundi, Afghanistan, Sudan and Somalia. The nature of the projects varied (police advice and mediation, assessment missions, DDR, post-conflict assistance, electoral assistance, etc.), but the emphasis was on short-term aid, either pre- or post-conflict, limited to six months. The special appeal of the RRM as a funding instrument, was that it could use fast-track procedures during critical phases of crisis situations and deliver rapidly. However, the fact that projects could only be supported for up to six months turned out to be a limiting factor in the RRM's effectiveness. Many post-conflict reconstruction projects need more time to come to fruition, and securing additional funding in such a short time proved difficult. Another issue was the connection between actions undertaken in the critical phase and actions to be undertaken in the mid-term stabilisation phase. RRM projects did not have sufficient duration to create a continuum with traditional /long-term rehabilitation support programmes managed by EuropeAid. Such concerns led to a further evolution in the way the EU considered its crisis response mechanisms.

On one side the European Council recognised in its conclusions of November 2004 that the effectiveness of EU external action is dependent on the **links between security and development**. This interdependence has been further recognised in the European Consensus on Development and the EU Strategy for Africa. On the other, notably as the result of the analysis of the global response to the Tsunami in 2004, the Commission launched a reflection[1] on issues of coordination, speed and usage of open source intelligence; all seen as critical factors to enhance EU's crisis response capacity.

The result of this process was the Instrument for Stability, which replaced the RRM in 2007, and which seeks to establish links between short-term crisis response and long term development assistance.

The Instrument for Stability is designed to allow the Community to respond urgently to the needs of countries threatened with or undergoing severe political instability or suffering from the effects of a technological or natural disaster in close co-ordination with Member States. Its purpose is to support measures aimed at safeguarding or re-establishing the conditions under which the partner countries of the EC can pursue their long term development goals. The main added value of the IfS is its ability to provide support to the political strategy of the Commission faced with a crisis in a third country.

While the IfS is a very flexible instrument, the Council Regulation establishing it imposes a number of legal constraints, notably:
- the maximum duration of any IfS project is 18 months;
- the IfS cannot finance humanitarian assistance;
- the IfS can only finance an operation where other EC instruments cannot respond within the timeframe necessary.

It should, moreover, be noted that a number of specialized financing instruments exist which have emergency provisions written into their legal basis allowing mobilisation of funds at short notice. They include the Regulations on:
- Food Aid
- Human Rights and Democratisation
- Mine Action
- Rehabilitation

The IfS may be triggered in situations of "crisis or emerging crisis, situations posing a threat to law and order, the security and safety of individuals, situations threatening to escalate into armed conflict or to destabilize the country". There are five essential conditions of deployment:
- **URGENCY.** The urgency of the situation is such that immediate action is required and other Community co-operation programmes are not able to respond.
- **POLITICAL PRIORITY.** The EU is actively engaged in the political process aimed at resolving conflict or defusing civilian crisis, or (in the case of other sudden-onset emergencies) the scale of the emergency is such that the effectiveness of the Community's long term co-operation programmes is jeopardised.
- **OPPORTUNITY.** A window of opportunity exists for a Community intervention, and conditions are sufficiently stable for deployment to be made with a reasonable level of risk.
- **EFFECTIVENESS.** The programme is sufficiently well-targeted to achieve its objectives within the 18 months period of IfS financing. These objectives must contribute to the preservation or re-establishment of the conditions of stability essential to the proper implementation and success of Community cooperation policies and programmes.

(1) With the Conference "From Needs to Solutions: enhancing the civilian crisis response capability of the European Union" organised in November 2005 together with the Crisis Management Initiative of President Martti Ahtisaari

- **FOLLOW-UP.** There is a readiness to adjust Commission country strategies and indicative programmes to take account of the circumstances that necessitate the deployment of the IfS. Where appropriate, follow-up measures will be financed and implemented rapidly under the medium and long-term Community co-operation programmes.

The IfS can be used in all areas of intervention that come under Community competence, with the exception of humanitarian assistance. This means that it can finance anything that can be financed from one of the geographical or horizontal financing instruments **without geographical restriction.**

The IfS will provide flexible Community assistance in:
- *assessment of possible Community responses to a crisis*. The IfS will deploy technical assessment missions in a range of areas in order to inform the Commission's policy making and planning during a crisis;
- *preventive action during emerging crises*. The IfS can finance short term actions as part of a wider package of Community and EU measures to address the immediate and root causes of an emerging crisis;
- *acute crisis management*. The IfS can be deployed during a conflict or in response to a sudden-onset emergency, to implement measures to restore stability;
- *post-conflict reconciliation*. The IfS can be used to provide confidence-building measures in support of an emerging or established peace process;
- *post-crisis reconstruction*. The IfS can be used to spearhead the long-term Community co-operation programmes in the immediate aftermath of a war or sudden-onset natural or man-made emergency, and to ensure a smooth transition between humanitarian relief operations, the re-establishment of civil administration and the rule of law, and subsequent rehabilitation and development programmes.

The IfS can also be used to pilot innovative approaches to addressing persistent instability in the EU's partner countries (for instance the development of medium term 'preventive strategies').

The key feature of IfS projects is the leverage effect they are intended to have. Leverage is measured both in terms of the impact on the process of stabilization, and in terms of bringing forward longer-term programmes using the larger financial resources available in the main EC geographical instruments.

By their nature, IfS projects may have a high degree of political risk, in particular where their implementation depends on the respect of the terms of peace agreement by parties to a conflict, or where the capacity of implementing partners is weak.

The Instrument for Stability has a significantly increased budget in comparison to its predecessor, and is used to fund and coordinate the whole array of EU crisis response tools — development, humanitarian, civilian and political — to attempt to eradicate global conflicts and crises from occurring or recurring.

Also, the European Commission has invested much effort into increasing the links between the institutions in Brussels that deal with crisis response, and reinforcing the operational links between all the Commission crisis rooms in Brussels, and between Brussels and Member State capitals.

INTERVIEW | CHRISTIAN BERGER
Head of the European Commission's
Crisis Response and Peace Building Unit

The Instrument for Stability dramatically increases the funds available to the European Commission for conflict prevention and crisis management. What are you going to do with these funds and how will it change the way you work?

The European Union is facing a number of challenges, such as dealing with crises and conflicts, addressing the disparity of wealth around the world — which in itself can be a root cause of conflicts — and managing natural resources in ways that do not lead to further conflicts. The European public expects us to respond to these challenges and the international community expects us to share the burden of international crisis management.

That's where we come in. The EU has a number of crisis response tools — humanitarian assistance, civil protection — providing assistance to countries hit by disasters and the military and police missions that are operated by Member States under the heading of the European Security and Defence Policy (ESDP).

The tool we are dealing with here is the Instrument for Stability (IfS), which replaces the Rapid Reaction Mechanism (RRM). Under that instrument we had a budget of roughly €30 million a year and now we have about €100 million a year, steadily rising to €400 million a year by 2013. So, combined with the budget for Member State operations under the CFSP we will have a budget of about €800 million by the year 2013 for the EU to respond to crisis situations, this in addition to the yearly €7- 8 billion for other external actions, such as humanitarian assistance, development co-operation and pre-accession.

Now, how are we going to use this extra money? Well, the first trigger for using the Stability Instrument is the opportunity of responding to an immediate crisis situation or trying to prevent a conflict from getting worse or breaking out. The second possibility is helping the international community to make use of a window of opportunity in a frozen conflict: for example, if there is a breakthrough in the Arab — Israeli peace talks the parties may ask the international community to underpin that agreement with specific actions. The third trigger is if the EU decides to deploy a police or military operation; there is often an opportunity for close co-operation. We are doing this in Chad, where the European military protects the civilian UN police mission, and the European Commission in turn funds the international component of that UN police operation. The fourth trigger is the need for help to recreate an environment conducive to long-term development taking root. For example, in Afghanistan, we have rule of law experts on the ground, who are working with the government to prepare a long-term law and justice mission.

How does this differ from what you were doing before?

Before it was more a reactive instrument, mainly trying to disburse funds quickly in response to a singular event. Now, the actions under the Stability Instrument are embedded in a broader response capacity of the European Union. As mentioned earlier, we now have more triggers for the Stability Instrument. Another major difference is that in the past we could only deploy for a maximum of six months, so it was really a short-term, immediate reaction. Now it is 18 months, so we can establish a close link between short-term emergency assistance and long-term development aid.

What spurred this change in strategy?

There was strong pressure from the European side — both civil society and governments — but also from our international partners, to do more, to be more present and to have more funds available for immediate crisis response.

We not only want to do more, we want to do it better. Our new approach is more coherent, by way of better co-ordination with our European and international partners — but also by ensuring that the different stages and phases of an intervention are well interlinked.

How do you cooperate with other international actors and how does the EU's approach to crisis prevention and management differ from them?

One thing is very clear — a single country, or the EU, cannot handle an international crisis on its own. You have to have a global approach and work very early in the crisis with international partners. Of course everyone follows their own strategies and applies their own rules and procedures but we have to make sure we coordinate very closely with each other. In fact, one of the features of the Stability Instrument is that we are implementing our programmes and projects with the help of others. In November 2007 we launched the idea of setting up a Peace-building Partnership through which we establish partnerships with the best-qualified organisations, agencies and think-tanks to work on crisis situations.

Isn't there are a risk that by involving so many partners your response will be slowed down?

I'm quite confident it won't slow it down and will, on the contrary, give us access to the best-qualified partners to work with. There is so much knowledge and expertise out there among NGOs, Member States and think-tanks that it would be unwise not to tap into those resources. It doesn't have to be a very complicated procedure — you call up those of your partners who have knowledge and expertise on the given issue, organise a brainstorming and draw on the valuable information these organisations have from working in the field.

Is there a specifically European approach to conflict prevention and crisis management, and what is the European value-added in dealing with these issues?

Why the European Union? Because it is regarded as a civilian power. That is an asset that makes it easier for the EU to engage with others because we are not seen as a body that wants to impose anything or that has a hidden agenda. Why the EU institutions? Because we work closely with all Member States have their political weight behind us which guarantees a greater impact.

In terms of a European approach to these issues, we know what the link is between security and development; they are two sides of the same coin and you can't have one without the other. People recognise we have a very strong developmental approach that can also have an impact on security. Others may have a different approach, placing security at the top of their agenda and focusing on how they can beef up security by providing development assistance. We believe it is ultimately the developmental approach that will boost stability.

With all these different bodies, both in and out of house, working to alleviate crisis situations and humanitarian disasters, isn't there a risk of duplication and overlap?

It works, but improvement is always possible. Michel Barnier drew up a report last year where he suggested there should be only one office dealing with humanitarian crises. At the moment you have ECHO (the European Commission Humanitarian Office) and the Commission civil protection office. He suggests replacing both with a one-stop shop.

Is the EU in a position to talk about conflict prevention, given its record in the Balkans, Rwanda and Darfur?

The EU is undertaking a vast range of activities in the field of conflict prevention. Assisting others in their efforts to carry out political and economic reforms, working with them on governance issues, human rights and democratisation, including election observation, but also on security sector reform and the rule of law have been important contributions to conflict prevention for many years. ESDP is a relatively new addition to the EU's foreign policy tools and the EU hasn't shied away from using it – some 17 or 18 times in fact, both military and civilian operations.

There is obviously an intrinsic, moral need to intervene in crisis situations, but are there any knock-on benefits for the EU in acting fast in terms of its image or standing?

A long-standing complaint of the European Union has been that it is a payer, but not a player. With these new instruments this is changing. The EU is becoming more and more involved in international affairs and not only as a donor. But visibility is still a problem and more needs to be done in this area. We need to explain why we are doing all this. First, I think it is because European public expects the EU to do more to make the world a little bit safer. But also when you improve your crisis response capability you also help European citizens who are stranded abroad in a conflict situation. Europeans make 180 million trips outside the EU each year and when you have a catastrophe like the 2004 tsunami, when you saw all these European citizens stranded in south-east Asia, you see a need for the EU to react faster, quicker and better.

Can you point to any outright successes the EU has had in the field, where you are personally proud of its response and follow-up?

Aceh in Indonesia is a good example of the European Union using the instruments it has in the right way. There, the European Commission supported the former Finnish President Martti Ahtissari in his efforts to negotiate a peace agreement. When that was signed, the EU Member States set up a mission to monitor the implementation of that agreement. Now the mission has come to an end but the European Commission is there to assist with the longer-term development of the country. So, I think Aceh has shown that there's no use stepping in quickly to stave off a conflict when the whole thing collapses again two years later.

Is this a job that keeps you awake at night, worrying when the next disaster will strike?

In the business of crisis response the stress level is pretty high, but when you see you can have positive results, when you know you have the tools and the support you need, you don't think "what will I do tomorrow if there's an earthquake?" It's more like "how can we do the job quickly and in close coordination with others?" The problem with crises and disasters is you can't foresee them, you can't programme your response in advance; so you have to take them as they come, but better make sure you are prepared.

AFGHANISTAN

Reform of the justice sector

REPORTAGE BY GARETH HARDING

PHOTOGRAPHS & CAPTIONS BY PAOLO WOODS

An Afghan family waits to be forcibly repatriated by Iranian authorities. In 2000 Iran hosted more than one million Afghan refugees that had escaped civil war, the Taliban repression and a very severe drought.
© Paolo Woods / Mashhad, Iran, 1999

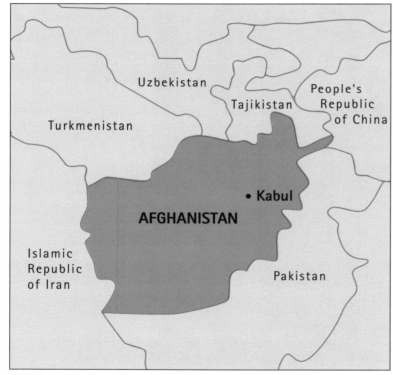

© GOPA-Cartermill

Capital: Kabul
Area: 645,807 km²
Population: 27,145,000 (2007)
Life expectancy at birth: male 43.2 years; female 43.5 years (2006)
Government type: Islamic republic with two legislative bodies
GDI – per capita: US$ 319 (2006)

Source: © 2008 Encyclopædia Britannica, Inc.

INTRODUCTION

In late 2001, following the fall of the Taliban, Afghanistan emerged from decades of occupation and warfare. Most of Afghanistan's physical and economic infrastructure was destroyed. Social development indicators ranked Afghanistan among the lowest in the world with respect to life expectancy and health. The Afghan people were deeply affected by ethnic strife. Afghanistan had all but ceased being a functioning state.

An international conference in December 2001 in Bonn brought the Afghan leadership and the international community together with the firm vision to bring stability, social and economic development to Afghanistan and help in building up its democratic institutions.

By 2008, Afghanistan has made much progress along this path. Milestones in this process were the adoption of the new constitution in January 2004, presidential elections in October 2004, parliamentary and provincial elections in September 2005 and the inauguration of the new National Assembly in December 2005. More than 80% of Afghanistan's population has access to primary health care, compared to coverage in 2001 of only 7%. Child mortality has dropped by over 25% in recent years, an important step for Afghanistan in reaching the Millennium Development Goals. The economy continues to grow at double digit rates and over 4,000 km of roads are now built, improving Afghanistan's trading capacity.

In a screening center of the Iranian authorities. Afghans that claim they cannot be repatriated due to ethnical and religious persecution by the Taliban, are interrogated here. Very few are granted the possibility to stay in Iran.
© Paolo Woods / Mashhad, Iran, 1999

An Afghan widow has just received a letter by the Iranian authorities that requires her to return to Afghanistan. Her husband has been killed by the Taliban for being a member of the Hazara ethnic minority. In 2000 Iran hosted more than one million Afghan refuges that had escaped civil war, the Taliban repression and a very severe drought.

© Paolo Woods / Mashhad, Iran, 1999

Yet Afghanistan still has a long way to go before it will finally overcome the heavy legacy of its past and make its democratic development sustainable. The resurgence of the Taliban in the course of 2007 has revealed the fragility of the Afghan state-building exercise. 2008 will be a challenging year, both for the Afghan government and the international community. The Afghan people will continue to show resilience as they have done in the past: government services are still not available throughout the country and regional integration has been slow; there is still uneven access to economic development and opportunities, making it difficult to wean parts of the country off the drugs economy. The international community will need to continue supporting the Afghans for the foreseeable future to ensure that Afghanistan continues on a path towards stability and prosperity.

Mullah Mohammad, a Taliban commander, runs the Mazlak refugee camp. His work mainly consists of quickly turning the international aid into profit for the Taliban. Each week Iran forcibly sends back about 5,000 Afghans. The refugees are supposed to then go on to their villages that were destroyed by war, plagued by drought and are now under the obscure control of the Taliban. However most of the refuges return illegally to Iran in the following weeks or just go on living in the Mazlak camp.
© Paolo Woods / Near Herat, Afghanistan, 2000

PROJECT FACTS & FIGURES

Programme
Afghanistan – Reform of the Justice Sector

Location
Afghanistan

Budget for IfS project
€1,350,000

Project start:
June 2007

Duration:
18 months

AFGHANISTAN AND THE EUROPEAN UNION

The European Union has been at the forefront of international efforts to bring stability, democracy and development to Afghanistan.

Twenty-five EU Member States are involved in the UN-sanctioned International Security Assistance Force (ISAF), which aims to provide the security needed for Afghanistan to develop. The 17,000 troops from EU nations account for around half of ISAF's total deployment. Several Member States are also contributing to the US-led Operation Enduring Freedom coalition conducting counter-insurgency and counter-terrorism operations in Afghanistan.

The European Union and its Member States collectively accounted for about 30 per cent of the US$12.5 billion in grants pledged by the international community for Afghan reconstruction at international conferences in Tokyo (2002) and Berlin (2004). At the London conference in spring 2006, the European Union pledged a further US$ 2.4 billion for reconstruction over the coming years.

EU aid has focused on building up shattered infrastructure such as roads, hospitals and schools, establishing new government institutions, reforming the public sector, promoting human rights, de-mining and providing alternative livelihoods for poppy farmers.

In addition to its leading role in the reconstruction effort, the European Union is a major source of emergency humanitarian aid. Total EU contributions for 2002–2006 amounted to €627.5 million.

The rule of law is critical for democracy to take root, for justice to be enforced, the economy to prosper and for drug barons to be defeated. Providing €205 million for the period 2003–2008, the European Union is the largest contributor to the Law and Order Trust Fund of Afghanistan, a key instrument which funds police salaries, training and procurement of equipment.

In addition, since June 2007 the European Union has run a police mission in Afghanistan which consists of some 160 police officers and aims to reform the country's police force.

An Afghan refugee girl in a NGO-run school near the refugee camp where she lives.
In the Taliban Afghanistan schooling for girls was forbidden and in Pakistan refugees
do not have access to education.
© Paolo Woods / Peshawar, Pakistan, 2001

PROJECT OBJECTIVES

To assist the Government of Afghanistan in strengthening the rule of law and providing an improved access to a formal justice system for citizens.

Among the programme's key aims:

- Help the Afghan government to draw up and implement a reform programme in institutions such as the Supreme Court and Attorney General's Office.

- Assist the government in developing a new legal aid system that provides a nationwide coverage of defence representation and improves access to a range of other mediation services.

REFORM OF THE JUSTICE SECTOR

In the current unstable and insecure environment of Afghanistan, the lack of a functioning rule of law represents one of the biggest challenges in the immediate period ahead. Without it, any long-term efforts to democratise and stabilise the country are likely to be redundant. In terms of human and physical resources, none of the judicial institutions are able to deliver an effective system of justice. Staff are inadequately trained, have no clear career structure and work in conditions of personal danger. Systems for the appointment, transfer and retirement of judges and prosecutors are ineffective and lack mechanisms for accountability and discipline. There is allegedly transparent widespread corruption. Unless the situation is urgently improved, there will be a significant threat to stability in Afghanistan.

Lawlessness and lack of recourse to a fair justice system have plagued Afghanistan for most of the last century. There is a deep-rooted distrust in and a reticence about using the formal judicial system, and sentences are often handed down and executed by individuals, village elders and tribal communities.

Even where there is a willingness to take a case to the formal system, there is very poor access to the courts system in many parts of the country. Corruption is endemic – partly because of low salaries in the sector – and no effective mechanisms exist for its detection and prosecution. This corruption is often expressed in a politicisation of the judiciary, where decisions of judges are frequently open to improper influence.

In addition to corruption, the failure to ensure a secure environment for courts, judicial personnel, victims and witnesses also contributes to undermining the capacity of the legal system to act independently and impartially. The result is a depressingly low level of public trust and confidence in the formal justice institutions.

Moreover, the absence of a strong independent bar and state-funded legal aid acts as a significant impediment to safeguarding the rights of accused persons and to providing the necessary legal representation for vulnerable groups. Traditional dispute resolution mechanisms, especially in rural areas, remain dominant. This is often to the detriment of women and children in particular.

Most critically, the justice system still lacks sufficiently qualified officials, adequate legal education, and the necessary administrative tools and infrastructure to administer justice properly, fairly or effectively. 50 per cent of prosecutors have not graduated from the faculties of law or Sharia. A similar picture emerges in the judiciary, with just over half of judges holding a law degree, 30 per cent of whom (15 per cent in total) are from religious schools. Around 20 per cent of existing judges were first appointed by the Taliban government.

The European Commission believes an effective justice system is a prerequisite for political, economic and social progress in Afghanistan. This is why the European Union is engaged in developing the Afghan National Police, fighting the illegal drugs trade and upholding basic human rights and the rule of law. But progress in any of these sectors necessitates a functioning justice system.

Some progress has been made in reforming Afghanistan's formal justice system. However, of all the sectors in Afghan public life, it remains perhaps the one in most urgent need of change.

The European Union's justice reform programme, through its team of locally based specialist staff, works closely with Afghan authorities to:
• set up an equitable salary structure within the Afghan judiciary to root out corruption
• establish clear timetables for existing judges and prosecutors to undergo the recruitment process
• develop a national legal aid programme, taking into account costs related to the recruitment and training of new defence lawyers.

The IfS project, which has an initial budget of €1.35 million, is seen as a first step towards a more root and branch reform of the justice system, which the Commission aims to support over the next few years.

A new wave of Afghan refugees has fled to Pakistan since the US-led attacks on the Taliban. Refugee camps are overcrowded. Here a family has found a safe haven in a relative's house.
© Paolo Woods / Peshawar, Pakistan, 2001

Afghan refugees work in carpet factories.
The carpet industry makes large use of child labour.
© Paolo Woods / Peshawar, Pakistan, 2001

| **PAUL TURNER**
Afghanistan Desk, EC Directorate-General
for External Relations

Building a fully functioning justice system in Afghanistan

If one talks to Afghans and people who have been involved in Afghanistan for a considerable time, they will say that during the period of the '70s prior to the Soviet invasion, there was something of a functioning justice system.

But one needs to keep in mind that there have always been three levels of justice. There are the secular and Sharia justice systems which together are the formal justice system. And then at the grass roots level there is the communal, village-based form of justice that has existed for centuries.

At present the more formal justice sector, whether secularised or Sharia, is either distrusted by or distanced from the population. Because of this distrust and inaccessibility, the vast of bulk of the population – over 80 per cent – uses the more communal-based justice system.

Our view across the international community has always been that there is a place for the traditional communal system – we are not trying to supersede it. I think, for example, in the areas of property rights and civil disputes the communal system should continue. In any case, the formal justice system hasn't got the resources to deal with every kind of case.

The problem comes when the communal system is seen to be exercising authority in an increasing number of criminal cases, for example murder or rape cases. Such cases are well documented of course with women's rights not being safeguarded.

Because the formal justice system has been so distant from the population and is often viewed as incompetent and corrupt, there is an urgent need to address how the mainstream judicial and public prosecution system functions. There are something like 1,500 judges in Afghanistan of which only 50 per cent have any formal degree, whether that's in Islamic or secular law; it gives you an idea of the challenges we've got.

Basic problems to address

First of all there is a lack of trust, and that stems from incompetence and corruption. Then there is a lack of physical infrastructure, courthouses and the like. After 30 years of war, the whole human and physical infrastructure of the justice sector has collapsed. The Rome Conference on Justice in July 2007 was a very useful forum in auditing these needs and prioritising donors' actions.

In terms of human resources, the European Commission is looking at recruitment systems, meritocratic promotion, codes of ethics and ultimately, pay and grading. In a sense everything is linked. We won't address corruption in the judiciary until we deal with pay. Today a judge gets US$50 a month. Clearly, that's inadequate and is just fostering corruption. So there is agreement that there has to be a whole rebalancing and reconsideration of what a decent pay level is for senior, middle-ranking judges. If we look at the police sector, a similar exercise has already been undertaken. We need to get a degree of parity in pay between the judiciary and police.

The EC will consider paying for enhanced justice salaries, as long as it goes in parallel with the whole justice reform process. In any case, the Afghans are determined to have a new law on salaries, which will cover judges' and politicians' pay.

The EU's role in reforming Afghanistan's justice system

First of all we need to get an agreement with the Supreme Court — which covers the 1,500 judges — and the Attorney General's office - which covers the 2,000 prosecutors — to actually understand the reforms that are needed. We have EC experts in the Supreme Court, the Attorney General's office and the Ministry of Justice, already talking with their Afghan interlocutors about new personnel and recruitment systems.

There is also the question of how you implement any new reforms: if I give you an example of the police, this was a difficult process. While there may have been police generals and colonels who were not fit to be in the service, one had to find interim arrangements for dealing with these groups. They continued to be paid their existing salaries, almost like a sort of redundancy pay, and at the same time new, younger, police officers who had passed the new recruitment process came into the service. We will need a similar implementation plan in the justice sector.

Can €1.35 million do all this?

Yes, but that is only financing the expert team out there now, which is a precursor to the main justice programme. The budget for this programme for the next three years will be in the region of €50–60 million. This amount of money could cover significant components of any enhanced salary system, clearly. But, again, this will depend on the reforms progressing. There are also other areas in the justice sector which our team is looking to support, in particular the setting-up of a new nation-wide legal aid system in Afghanistan. There are many provinces where not even one defence lawyer resides, an indication of how remote the formal legal system is from the ordinary Afghan's day to day life.

Making the justice sector a priority

I think in post-conflict or ongoing conflict situations like we've got in Afghanistan, the temptation of donors is to have an emergency 'paramedic' sort of mentality and overlook the more structural elements. In fact, when we were coming out of the immediate post-war situation in Afghanistan — by which I mean when the Taliban was defeated — there was a need to build up central structures and to address the opium trade, and to do this effectively you needed a functioning justice system.

The justice sector was overlooked in the aftermath of the conflict, partly perhaps because it's the most difficult sector to address. And yet it does underpin everything. Opinion polls seem to show that most Afghans are worried about their own personal security. One of the top concerns they cite is corruption and no right of redress through the legal system. Justice is always high on the list of concerns.

Linking the justice reform and police reform programmes

The Commission has been a major funder of the so-called Law and Order Trust Fund (LOTFA), which has been paying police salaries. From 2002–2008 we have put over €200 million into LOTFA, which the EU is increasingly using as a tool to further the necessary reforms in the Afghan National Police and the Ministry of Interior.

The link between our work in the police and justice sectors is clear. What the EU is aiming to do is look at the whole rule of law sector more holistically. An example is the public prosecution system. The Commission is dealing with institutional reform of the public prosecution system, its personnel systems, recruitment systems etc. Meanwhile, the new EUPOL police mission is looking at the prosecution service in terms of its linkage to the police at an

Afghan refugees fleeing the US-led attacks on the Taliban find shelter inside a mosque.
© Paolo Woods / Peshawar, Pakistan, 2001

operational level. So we're trying to get a more holistic approach in terms of their dealing with how the police dovetails with the criminal justice system through the public prosecution service.

EU support resulting in advancements for Afghanistan

I think there are now genuine improvements in terms of the structure of the police. There are still problems in the rank and file but the structure of the police, the new systems of recruitment, pay and grading, and vetting process for the senior ranks represents progress. We need to keep up with the reforms across the police service and start now on the justice sector.

More generally, where I think there has been success is in the so-called 'soft sectors', particularly education and health, which you wouldn't have read much about because they've been overshadowed by the other news. Some 90,000 children are alive today in Afghanistan who wouldn't have been seven years ago, and infant and maternal mortality is still coming down. There are six million children in primary school, of which two million are girls. Now these are achievements since 2002 that don't really make the newspapers.

I have personally witnessed both good and bad changes in the years I've been going to Afghanistan. Good, particularly in the health sector for example and there are advances in other economic sectors too. Negative changes – I think it is difficult to deny that the security situation in Kabul and in other areas has now significantly deteriorated. My first ever trip was in April 2005. I remember being able to walk in the centre of Kabul relatively easily, which would not be possible now. The difference now is that the conflict has now come to Kabul and spread to other areas beyond the south.

Prospects for the future

Ultimately I think the insurgency could be one of these drawn-out stalemates. But, asked the question, 'can Afghans start to have more faith in how the state and the government work for them?' I would answer 'Yes, in time.' I also think the war on the opium trade is winnable.

The insurgency is a real problem however and it seems to have taken on more menacing features. But there are plenty of countries that survive with a continual security threat. For example, Sri Lanka has an ongoing security problem. Bombs occasionally go off in Colombo. But the government apparatus of the Sri Lankan state still functions.

The problem in Afghanistan at the moment is that were the international community to leave, the country would not be able to cope with the insurgency. This is the challenge: we need to get to a point where the Afghan nation state can deal with an ongoing security problem in a part of its territory without the whole state being threatened. We are not there yet but the development of the Afghan National Army has been a success story to date and this is heartening to see.

A final point. We need to keep in mind that some 80 per cent of Afghans still want foreign soldiers there to protect them. The Taliban are not, as Chairman Mao would have said, 'fish swimming in friendly seas'. They operate on the basis of fear and intimidation in the local communities. There's not a deep-rooted level of support for them. We sometimes lose track of this and exaggerate their support and significance.

At a brick factory in the outskirts of Peshawar,
an Afghan refugee listens to the radio news about the US-led attacks on the Taliban.
© Paolo Woods / Peshawar, Pakistan, 2001

INTERVIEW | **MIKE SAN AGUSTÍN MCCREA**
Crisis Response Planner
EC Directorate-General for External Relations

The Afghanistan Justice Sector Reform Project was designed in the context of the serious thrust to make law and order a reality for the "Afghan in the street". The project had to assist the government to bring the key institutions – the Court System, Prosecution Services, and indeed the Ministry of Justice – from their impoverished state after the departure of the Taliban from central government, to a level where there is an effective treatment of criminal cases, from detection through to sentencing, and beyond.

There were already activities supporting the institutions of law and order before this programme came along. The EC had already been contributing a considerable amount to a trust fund for Police salaries, and a major European Security and Defence Policy programme to support the Afghan National Police Force to fulfil its role in a civilian environment was established in parallel to this project. Other donors were also active in the same field. The challenge was to usefully contribute, without stepping on toes, or devaluing the work of others because of philosophical differences.

So going back to basics, we looked at some of the questions faced by all administrations: what type of staff is required; what qualifications, training and experience do they have; is it appropriate; and whether they are realistically recompensed for what they do, or should be doing.

Bear in mind that when the project began the average salary of a judge, of whom 20% had at the most a secondary school education, was about €60 a month! Prosecutors earned even less, about €40. Those who live in some locations outside Kabul often had to contend with an environment where an inappropriate decision could cost them their lives.

One other area which had been left untouched by other actors was the question of access to justice, and in particular the system of legal aid available to Afghans unable to finance the costs of defence in courts themselves.

The EC project is hoping to ensure that all the justice institutions will have effective staff records, job descriptions with appropriate minimum qualification requirements, a clear and transparent salary scale to reduce temptation for dishonest activities, and an appointments system to ensure that new staff have the appropriate qualifications, training and experience for the job. The project has a particular focus on those legal staff who do not fall directly under the Civil Service legislation, such as the 1,700 judges and the 2,500 prosecutors.

Support for the capacity of the institutions to draw up budgets and obtain approbations meant that these units were for the first time able to draw up well-argued proposals for their 2008 budget. This work, of course, involves other government departments, including the Civil Service Commission, and the Ministry of Finance.

Much of the support is to assist the administration to develop innovative working methods, such as working groups on specific issues. Project staff provide information on how other countries deal with similar issues, and provide training on issues ranging from computer systems and file management to expenditure controls.

This programme has a limited lifetime, and is just a start in many of these processes. A follow-up is expected in the future. Some planning is under way, which will use the evaluation of progress made under this programme.

At the frontline between Jamiat and Jumbesh militias.
Adan Khan, 28 years old (centre) is a Jamiat soldier, responsible for this outpost.
A recent Jumbesh offensive has forced them to make a 4 kilometre retreat.
© Paolo Woods / Near Balkh, Afghanistan, November 2003

INTERVIEW | BETTINA MUSCHEIDT
Afghanistan Desk, EC Directorate-General
for External Relations

Afghanistan today and in the past

Compared with a decade or so ago Afghanistan in many respects is a totally changed country. If you go back in history you will see there has never been a strong central government providing services to citizens. And while we're still very far from reaching our targets, considerable progress has been made in many fields. Much of this progress has been overlooked — understandably so — because people are very impatient.

If you compare Afghanis' access to health, education and basic government services to other people round the world you are likely going to be disappointed. However, very few Afghans had access to healthcare under the Taliban or previous governments. Now it is widely considered to be one of the most important achievements that over 80 per cent of the population has a primary healthcare centre within an hour-and-a-half to two hours' walking distance of where they live.

Health is a success story in Afghanistan under the Karzai administration because in recent years we've saved the lives of 40,000 infants annually in comparison with previous times because mothers now have access to healthcare. We have thereby already reduced child mortality by 25 per cent, though Afghanistan's child mortality still remains one of the highest in the world. Within the next years we believe we can get pretty close to 100 per cent access to primary healthcare, and future EC programmes will look at strengthening secondary healthcare in an affordable way.

Dog fights in one of Kabul's suburbs. Afghans are particularly keen on animal fights, which normally take place on Fridays. Big crowds gather to see and bet on the fights. Each dog represents one of the neighbourhoods of Kabul, its supporters cheer for that particular dog. As the Kabul neighbourhoods are strongly ethnically, religiously and economically divided these fights somehow reenact the long civil war that has ripped the country into pieces in the 1990s.
© Paolo Woods / Kabul, Afghanistan, November 2003

A crowd gathers to celebrate No Ruz, the Afghan new year. It is 1381 in their calendar.
It is the first time in years that the members of the Shia community can freely celebrate this festivity
of Persian origin that was repressed during the Taliban regime.
© Paolo Woods / Kabul, Afghanistan, 21st of March 2002

Yet there are still many burning issues still to tackle

We always have to remember where we started from, and it's very important we do not overlook the successes. But let me turn to the less rosy part of the picture.

For very clear historic reasons, the government still remains weak in the provinces and many government institutions and functions need strengthening. The Afghan parliament is young and the development of a party democracy has yet to come. Afghanistan's judiciary must become more professional to ensure that Afghans have real trust in their justice system. Afghans themselves will need to tackle many questions in the next years.

Some of them will be very painful – firstly, how to deal with transitional justice and how to achieve national reconciliation – after so much pain inflicted on this population.

The government, with the help of the international community, is pursuing a new order after the fall of the Taliban – Afghans will need to assess whether it is worthwhile supporting this state-building process: Can the country afford to further delay complete disarmament of illegally armed groups? Should Afghanistan be a country with free media and lively public debate generating ideas to help the country move forward? Or should those who express their opinion freely be prosecuted? How should nominations for senior positions in government be handled? Are transparency and accountability of government functions important? How much longer can Afghanistan afford a gender policy that still mostly excludes half of its population and its potential to take the country forward?

These are just a few questions not only Afghans but also outside observers might raise when looking ahead. One thing we cannot take away from the Afghans is responsibility. The international community and the European

Commission with it can assist but Afghans increasingly need to determine the course themselves. It is their country that needs to be built.

But I have no doubt that this situation is evolving all the time – you can see how much the Afghans themselves wish to move forward. Now comes the big question: it will take much time before Afghanistan has caught up with other parts of the world and such a long process will need stamina, both from the Afghans and the international community. Understandably, Afghans are impatient, as they rightly feel that they have, in the past decade, lost out on very basic human rights; those related to social and economic development, and also many individual rights.

Hopes for peace
I think that no place is eternally condemned to conflict. Look at Europe that used to be at war for centuries but thanks to the European integration most of our continent has enjoyed lasting peace for more than 60 years now.

But certainly countries that are forgotten by the world community can slip. I don't think that the world should ever allow Afghanistan to slide back into the obscurity the country experienced for decades because, in today's globalised world, we cannot afford one member of the global community to get so weak that it becomes a haven for terrorists and illicit crops.

Overcoming the natural antipathy to foreign-imposed rule
I think that this time the parameters are rather different. And so far the Afghan population has recognised that. Past foreign interventions were rather one-sided – often more geared at subjugating the Afghan people, controlling resources, trade routes etc. Basically nobody has ever come with the aim of improving the lives of Afghanis.

This passage in the Hindu Kush was built in 1964 by the Soviets in the name of the "friendship between nations". Fifteen years later it allowed them to invade the country more rapidly. It has been the borderline between the Taliban and the Northern Alliance and frequently mined and boomed. Now cars get stuck in the pavement holes or blocked by the ice and travellers often die of asphyxia in this dark and stuffy tunnel.
© Paolo Woods / Inside the Salang Tunnel, Afghanistan March 2002

If you look at public opinion surveys you will find that the overwhelming attitude of the Afghans is still 'We want the international community here. We do believe that the international community can contribute to improving our lives. Perhaps these improvements are not happening fast enough but we do want to see better government. We certainly don't want to see the kind of modernity you see in other countries, even in other Asian countries. But we do want to have what most people around the world strive for – a peaceful life that allows you to pursue your potential.' That is probably the most important reason that today's intervention is not doomed in Afghanistan.

Military efforts or development work?

There was a lot of criticism in the course of 2007 – a year that saw a particularly high number of civilian casualties as a result of the military's aerial campaign. But it is important not to forget how many civilian casualties were actually caused by the Taliban.

Now does the military effort cancel the development work out? I do not think so. We certainly have to become faster and better at delivering aid. But the Afghan government must also do its share. It needs to become more effective – to make the best use of the resources the international community can bring.

There are many difficulties to overcome for Afghans, notably that of the human resource basis. During such a long time of conflict education was obviously neglected and a lot of catching up needs to be done. This will need time. It may also imply changing attitudes and Afghans will have to ask themselves again questions such as whether girls should go to school and pursue further education or not, even if it would mean that they would have to move to the next town.

At the same time, with the development process moving on, the Afghan government will need to make judicious decisions on matters I have already mentioned. As I said, it concerns appointing the right, qualified people to senior positions in provincial and central governments but also striving for transparent and accountable government functions. I say this bearing in mind that it is the Afghan people who will judge the performance of their own government.

Delivering aid in volatile areas

We will always need to adapt the way we deliver aid. But when asked whether we can continue to operate under present circumstances, I point out that for the last five or six years, we have been committing 80 per cent of our funds per year and disbursements continue apace. We do this by working closely with Afghan partners who can reach parts of the country where foreigners find access more difficult. We also use trust funds managed by the UN or World Bank to strengthen central government functions

The bottom line is that we will not allow the country to slip back into a situation where the investment we've all made – and I'll start with the investment the Afghans themselves have made risking their health and even paying with their lives – is allowed to unravel and slip back. For the region it is utterly important to make Afghanistan a stable country, so there is no question of allowing the militants and insurgents to derail the overall aid effort.

Heading in the right direction and making a real difference

When I talk to friends and family back home in Germany, who are taxpayers, I frequently come across questions whether I feel the EU is heading in the right directions and if I feel I make a difference with my work. For the European Commission I think the overall picture is not negative, if I look at what we've done and what we set out to do.

First, as already mentioned, the Commission has been one of the three main donors in the health sector. It's a clear success and one upon which we can build.

Since the Taliban have been defeated the UN has decided that all Afghan children have to attend school. But in most villages there are no schools left. Here in Arab Arzai 400 kids learn sitting on the grass. Not only the facilities are missing there are no teachers left either. The students that know how to read try to teach the ones that don't.
© Paolo Woods / Arab Arzai, Afghanistan, April 2002

Secondly, we have over the last years made a clear difference in the field of providing alternative livelihoods in all of the provinces in the East of the country where we are engaged. We have seen very positive trends and a pretty complete rolling back of the opium industry, basically because in these regions we have helped provide alternative economic opportunities, plus better governance. There has been one exception though which we, the European Commission, are now tackling – in the past not enough attention was paid to the country's justice system, to the institutions that represent the state towards the citizen. Looking to the future, I do believe that the Commission is on track when you look at justice reform, and that you can do a lot more to improve the credibility of the Afghan state towards its citizens. Professional justice institutions would go a long way, including the ability to deliver legal aid, so that would be my third point.

Concerns for the country

What keeps me up at night are the violent attacks and some of the stories you catch in the papers. I just read that the film The Kite Runner has been forbidden in Afghanistan. Then there was the photo of that Afghan girl, barely a teenager, looking more than bewildered, frightened because she was newly wed to a much older husband, to whom she had been traded. So: the fact that many people are not seeing their basic rights realised, that there may be a roll-back of whatever rights they have acquired in recent years. That we are not able to reach people and to convince them this is not the way to go and that they are doing tremendous harm to their own society, is something I find extremely worrying. I also find it disturbing that we cannot convince enough of the armed factions to come into the fold.

These are indeed very, very worrying factors. But they also inspire us to work harder to deliver what the Afghan people deserve after waiting such a long time for better life conditions.

The UN have sent Shamsuddine and his family back to his village from the refuge camp in Mazlak where they had sought protection from the war and the drought. They were given one sack of wheat to eat and one to sow. It is not the sowing season so after the first sack was finished they ate the second. Now they eat wild grass.
© Paolo Woods / Kharestan-Idriss, Afghanistan, April 2002

INTERVIEW | BEREND DE GROOT
Head of Operations,
EC Delegation to Afghanistan

The current situation in Kabul

It always amazes me to hear that things are so poor in Afghanistan, but if you see the economic life in towns like Kabul, it's actually incredibly lively and bustling.

On the other hand, when it comes to the security side, of course, we all know about the threats that are there. We know from our own staff that when you go into these bustling areas of the town security is a serious issue and remains a serious issue.

From a security point of view the overall feeling is that the situation is not improving. When you talk about livelihoods, what people mention is that in the last few months, food prices have risen substantially. The causes are several. One is the world market price for food like grain, which is increasing. The situation in Pakistan is also playing a role in pushing up prices. This is something which rightly worries the government, however it just stresses even more the need to accelerate the development process.

The European Union making a difference

There are number of sectors where there has been significant progress. Donor contributions have succeeded in getting the basic health system reasonably back on track. In agriculture, there has been a substantial contribution in a number of sectors. We are making quite a bit of investment in the renovation and expansion of irrigation schemes, which is resulting in a very fast and visible improvement for farmers. We are also funding a major project to provide seeds to farmers, which has been supporting an increase in agricultural production.

On the governance side, we can mention the construction of a customs crossing to Pakistan, which is the major customs office in the region. Next we are looking to the north, to Tajikistan and after that we hope to do the same for the border with Uzbekistan. This will make a strong contribution to the tax income. This is extremely important.

Turning to the police, the European Union has been a major contributor to the Law and Order Trust Fund, which provides for the salaries of the Afghan police force and provides an important basis for the ongoing police reforms.

Putting in place a functioning justice system

There is a Supreme Court. There is an Attorney General's office. There is a Ministry of Justice. There are courts. There are judges. However, there is a tremendous job to be done. The qualifications of many people in the system, by international standards, ranks as insufficient. Coming out of a war situation means that in all these institutions there is an enormous history of backlog of investments, whether we talk about buildings, qualified human resources or ways of working. It's all very, very basic.

The men of Amanullah Khan standing on a tank they have recently conquered from the troops of Isamel Khan in Herat. The war of factions opposing Amanullah Khan and Isamel Khan is one of the many that still prevents Afghanistan from returning to peace. Warlords like Amanullah Khan thrive on this. Amanullah Khan is a Pashto warlord in control of the valley of Zirku just under Herat. He has been a Taliban and is now seeking collaboration with the central government of Hamid Karzai.
© Paolo Woods / Shindand, Afghanistan, November 2003

On 'TV hill', one of the hills overlooking Kabul, a boy swings from the dangling electric wires
of a pylon destroyed by the war.
© Paolo Woods / Kabul, Afghanistan, November 2003

Towards a better future

You have to be careful of looking at Afghanistan and expecting that if today we start investing then tomorrow we'll have this nicely functioning country. You have to see it very much as a process with a time horizon of 10 - 20 years. It's a situation where you have to make a start by making a number of investments. But you also need a mentality change, which is something that will take quite a bit of time and can only take place when the environment is conducive.

In a situation where security was not the problem that it is today, I would expect a number of programmes to go substantially more smoothly. And of course funding would also be more efficient. We believe that the only way forward is to stabilise the country and then get it back on a development path. For over 30 years Afghanistan has effectively been bombed back into medieval times, and in the process it has lost a lot of its capacities. This will take a substantial time to turn around, even with the current volume of Western engagement.

Finding motivation

I've been working for a long time in the development sector. I think, from a purely professional point of view, for me Afghanistan is a motivating area to be engaged in. When people ask, 'Why are you risking your life on this?' I admit there are certain risks. That's undeniable. On the other hand, there are also risks elsewhere and, as it stands, I find it doable.

CHAD

Boosting security in refugee camps

REPORTAGE BY CHRIS COAKLEY

PHOTOGRAPHS & CAPTIONS BY – ALVARO YBARRA ZAVALA

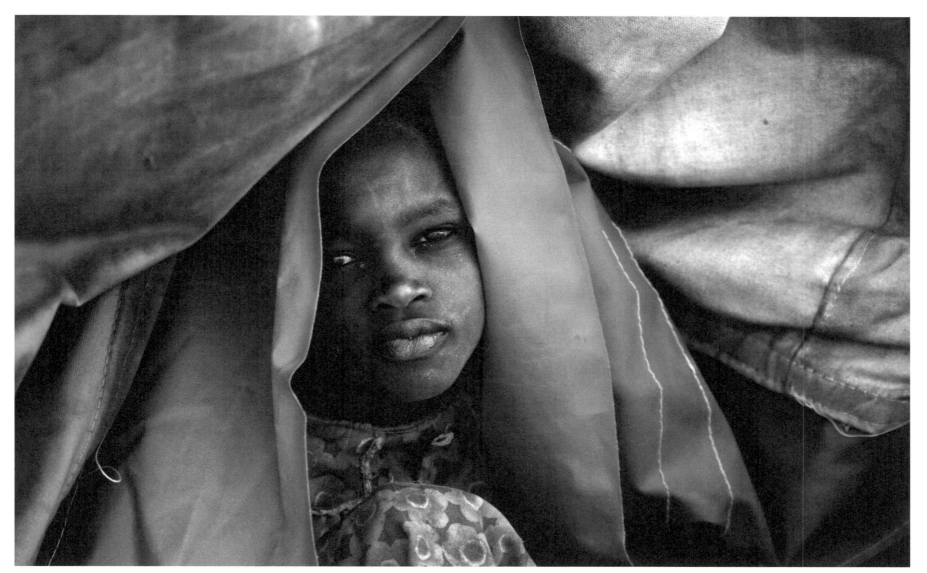

The refugee camps set up in Chad are all full of war orphans.
© Alvaro Ybarra Zavala / Agence VU / Chad

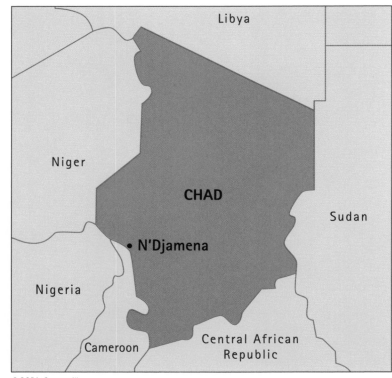

© GOPA-Cartermill

Capital: N'Djamena

Area: 1.284 million km²

Population: 10,239,000 (2007)
note: Excludes about 235,000 Sudanese refuees in eastern Chad in mid-2007.

Life expectancy at birth: male 45.6 years; female 48.9 years (2005)

Government type: unitary republic with one legislative body

GNP – per capita: US$ 335 (2006)

Source: ©2008 Encyclopædia Britannica, inc.

INTRODUCTION

Chad gained independence in 1960, having been first a colony and later an 'overseas territory' of France. The early years of Chad's independence were however blighted by an armed revolt and guerrilla war in the north of the country. Libya supplied weapons to insurgents in this area, annexed part of the territory and later supported the presidency of Goukouni Oueddei, who assumed power in 1979.

Hissene Habre, a former prime minister of Chad, took power in the early 1980s and reclaimed the northern region annexed by Libya. In turn, he was defeated by the army of Idriss Déby, who took power in 1990 and remains president to this day. Déby reopened the multi-party system in 1992 after 30 years of one-party rule. He won presidential elections in 1996, 2001 and 2006, although the validity of the results has been strongly contested by opposition groups.

Two major armed rebellions took place around the turn of the century. In 1998, a former minister in Déby's government launched an armed rebellion under the banner of 'Movement for Democracy and Justice'. Libya brokered a peace deal between the government and rebels in 2002. The deal did not conclude hostilities and the Chadian government was faced by another rebellion in the east by the National Resistance Army.

Instability in eastern Chad

There is a long history of tensions and conflict between different ethnic groups in eastern Chad. Even given this background, the

The 600 km territory ranging from the common border is a vast area to cover in case of emergency. Many of the refugees who manage to cross the border remain isolated in the desert for weeks without any kind of help until the the UNHCR staff locate them and take them to the camps.
© Alvaro Ybarra Zavala / Agence VU / Chad

45

TIMELINE

1960 Chad gains independence from France

1990 Idriss Déby assumes power

1992 A multi-party system of government is opened for the first time since the early years of independence

1996 Idriss Déby is elected and continues as president

1998 The 'Movement for Justice' armed rebellion begins. Peace deals are later signed in 2002 and 2003

2001 Idriss Déby is re-elected as president for a second five-year term

2003 Chad joins the community of oil exporting nations, as a pipeline to Cameroon is completed

2004 Refugees from the Darfur area of Sudan begin to cross the border into Chad en masse. Clashes ensue between government forces and pro-Sudanese armed groups

2006 April: A coup is narrowly averted as rebel groups reach the outskirts of N'Djamena

  May: Idriss Déby is re-elected as president amid boycotts from opposition parties

2007 The United Nations reports attacks on civilians early in the year

  September: UN Resolution 1778 is adopted, which makes a commitment to the protection of refugees and the local population, and details the supporting role to be played by the European Union

2008 28 January: EU foreign ministers give a green light to the deployment of 3,500 EUFOR troops to support the UN mission. Deployment started immediately

  1 February: deployment suspended due to fights between government forces and rebels in N'Djamena. This has worsened the Chad-Sudan relations and resulted in a declared state of emergency and the arrest of political opponents

  10 February: Deployment of 250 Special Forces

The long wait receiving food is part of the daily life in the Chadian refugee camps. Without the humanitarian help it would be nearly impossible for the refugees to survive.

© Alvaro Ybarra Zavala / Agence VU / Chad

security situation is seen to have degenerated in recent years. The breakdown is linked to the catastrophic situation in the neighbouring Darfur region of Sudan. More than 200,000 refugees have crossed the border and now live in camps close to local populations in eastern Chad.

Some warlords from Chad have supported the Sudanese government in targeting rebels in the Darfur area. There have also been incursions of armed bands from Darfur, attacking civilians and committing atrocities in eastern Chad. This has been a key factor in displacing members of the local population, whose numbers are estimated at around 180,000.

Tensions have risen between refugees in camps and nearby local populations. There have also been tensions between different refugees, internally displaced persons and the various ethnic groups within the camps.

An International Crisis Group report of June 2006 noted the spillover effect from Darfur but also pointed to the 'political crisis of the semi-authoritarian regime' in Chad as a contributing factor to the instability in its eastern region.

Oil reserves and the economic situation

In 2003, Chad became an exporter of oil when a new pipeline linked to Cameroon to the south. The emerging oil industry has been characterised by the joint involvement of the Chadian government, oil companies and the World Bank.

The World Bank made the initial investment of US$ 190 million to start the project on condition that the lion's share of oil revenues would be spent on programmes to reduce poverty. These included education, health and rural development projects. A government amendment to this deal led to a dispute with the World Bank. This has now been largely resolved and under Chadian budget law, at least 70 per cent of oil revenues must be earmarked for development spending.

Despite the emergence of oil revenues, Chad ranks among the ten poorest nations in the world according to the UN Human Development Index. It also ranks among the ten most corrupt nations according to Transparency International's Corruption Perceptions Index. Chad's human rights record and its judiciary sector have come under particular criticism in recent years.

THE EUROPEAN AND INTERNATIONAL RESPONSE

The European Union is the primary trade partner of Chad, whose main export is cotton. Europe is also the most important provider of development aid. In 2002, a total of €273 million was earmarked under the Ninth European Development Fund.

Chad has also received EU humanitarian aid funding. In 2006, ECHO (the European Union's humanitarian aid office) allocated €14 million to projects supporting refugees, returnees and local people. These funds are targeted towards food, water sanitation, education and healthcare services in particular.

A number of non-government organisations (NGOs) and civil society organisations are active in Chad. For example, Amnesty International was instrumental in reporting on the deteriorating situation and armed incursions of Janjaweed bands in 2006. Since 2004, Oxfam has played a key role in improving water, sanitation and public health in refugee camps. Humanitarian assistance in Chad received some unwelcome headlines in October 2007 when members of a French non-government organisation (NGO) were arrested on suspicion of illegally abducting children for adoption.

The situation in eastern Chad threatens the stability of the wider country, the security of the civilian population and the conduct of humanitarian efforts in the area. International response to this is defined largely by UN Security Council Resolution 1778, adopted on 25 September 2007.

The Resolution sets out the commitment to the protection of refugees and the local population and to uphold human rights and the rule of law. To this end, it establishes the deployment of a UN-EU presence in Chad, which has been approved by the European Union and Chadian government.

Specifically, the United Nations Mission in the Central African Republic and Chad (MINURCAT) sets out to train local police to patrol the camps and establish police cooperation, which will be supported by the European Commission and funded through the Instrument for Stability (IfS). MINURCAT also authorises a EU military force (EUFOR) to protect civilians, give cover to UN personnel and operations, and facilitate the delivery of humanitarian aid.

Chad is at a crossroads in 2008. This year presents a window of opportunity to stabilise the situation in the eastern region and defuse ethnic tensions. Success depends on multiple factors, but effective implementation of the UN resolution is key. A longer-term solution will depend on securing the domestic political situation (with a particular emphasis on free and fair elections in 2009) and also on finding a lasting resolution to the situation in neighbouring Darfur.

PROJECT FACTS & FIGURES

Programme
EU Military Operation in Eastern Chad and North Eastern Central African Republic (EUFOR TCHAD/RCA)

Locations
Eastern Chad and North Eastern Central African Republic

Total eligible cost
€99.2 million

Total amount sponsored by the EU
€50 million

Budget for IfS project
up to €10 million

Partners
UN Security Council, United Nations Mission in the Central African Republic and Chad (MINURCAT)

Project start
On 10 February 250 Special Forces were deployed

Duration
12 months

The refugee camps set up in Chad are all full of war orphans.
© Alvaro Ybarra Zavala / Agence VU / Chad

PROJECT OBJECTIVES

**Bridging Military Operation —
an interim operation designed to
support the multi-dimensional United
Nations presence in the east of Chad
and in the north-east of the Central
African Republic in order to improve
security in those regions.**

Specific objectives:

- To contribute to protecting civilians
  in danger, particularly refugees and
  displaced persons.

- To facilitate the delivery of
  humanitarian aid and the free
  movement of humanitarian personnel
  by helping to improve security in the
  area of operations.

- To contribute to protecting UN
  personnel, facilities, installations and
  equipment and to ensure the security
  and freedom of movement of its staff
  and UN and associated personnel.

All over the border with Chad thousands of villages have been destroyed by the armed gunmen – Janjaweed.
© Alvaro Ybarra Zavala / Agence VU / Sudan, near Kutum

INTERVIEW | **EDUARD AUER**
Crisis response planner, EC Directorate-General for External Relations

Launching an IfS project in Chad

In 2007, UN reports pointed to a deterioration of the security situation in eastern Chad. There was an increasing level of violence involving refugees, who number around 200,000 in this area. Furthermore the risk of spillover from the conflict in neighbouring Darfur threatened to make the situation even more problematic.

On 25 September 2007 the UN Security Council adopted Resolution 1778 to establish a mission in Chad. This was the defining moment for EU involvement, as it gave a mandate to the European Union to launch a military mission in the country.

In addition, there were a number of attacks on the civilian population by armed bands. The result is that there are a number of internally displaced persons (IDPs) as well as the refugees from Darfur in the camps. There have been tensions between the different groups in the camps, and also between refugees and the local population.

The European Union's role in a military operation

Following an initial crisis assessment, the United Nations planned to tackle the problem with an integrated mission involving a whole spectrum of UN actors. The first element was a civilian police force for the refugee camps that would include not only international police but also trained local officers. In parallel there would be a political representative in the capital. The other part of the initial idea was to deploy a UN blue-helmet military operation.

The government of Chad accepted the plans for the police and political representative but objected to the presence of UN soldiers. It became clear however that it would accept EU soldiers. That is why the UN Resolution provided for an EU force to secure the countryside and the areas outside the refugee camps, and to back up police within the camps where needed. The civilian aspect is to be handled by the United Nations.

The European Commission could clearly not participate in the military side, but we saw an opportunity to work together with the United Nations on the civilian part. This is the course of action we decided to take, with actions funded under the IfS.

The European Union and United Nations cooperation

The European Union and United Nations work together very well in many situations. We share a common view on how conflicts should be tackled, as well as a strong commitment to national governments and the rule of international law. We have a strong and very positive cooperation in many areas of the world.

This particular project in Chad is quite innovative in that it appears to be the first time that the European Union will provide military cover for a UN mission. This raises several issues, such as meeting UN expectations in terms of protection guarantees for its civilian workers. There is also the question of military logistics. Of course, discussion is required to agree on a modus operandi, and close cooperation will need to continue throughout the mission. So far the cooperation has been very positive, and the Chad mission could one day serve as a model for future operations.

On the border between Chad and Sudan international NGOs help taking the refugees to a safe place.
© Alvaro Ybarra Zavala / Agence VU / Chad

The European Commission's role

The European Commission is engaged in two operations in cooperation with the United Nations. The first is to support the UN deployment of the Chadian Police for Humanitarian Protection (PTPH).

The second is to prepare for the elections in 2009. We shall take care of the electoral census and voter registration. This is part of our efforts to help with the various political problems. The head of the Commission office in Chad was instrumental in brokering an agreement for free and fair elections in 2009, signed by the government and the legal opposition.

The European Commission has worked with the United Nations on projects in many other areas and has established processes. I believe, though, that this is one of the first times we have implemented a project together with the Department for Peace-keeping Operations. So in that sense the cooperation is a new experience for both sides.

We have formalised our cooperation with the United Nations, and signed contracts for both the support to police and electoral preparations in December 2007. However these two UN projects are not all we do in Chad. We have a long history of providing development assistance, and more recently, also humanitarian assistance.

Giving police training

There will be a three-step approach for the police training. Firstly, the Chadian police forces will propose candidates to the United Nations, who will select those most suited. After the selection process, around 100–200 police will be trained in the first month. After four to six months, the target strength of 850 will be reached.

A lady at the first aid post near the Bahai refugee camp.
© Alvaro Ybarra Zavala / Agence VU / Chad

Training will be run by African and international experts, with the aim of giving skills needed to work in refugee camps, such as riot control techniques. Human rights issues will also be part of the training. This will be a new element for nearly all the officers, since this is not a standard element of training in the Chadian police.

The police will be equipped and deployed for a six-month period before they return to their original units. They will receive a stipend superior to their usual pay. Then a new batch will be trained. In this way, a very substantial number of officers will be trained in modern policing techniques over a three-year period.

This approach of the United Nations merges two objectives. Firstly it makes it possible to deploy local people in camps. They are from different ethnic groups among the IDPs and refugees. They are more accustomed to local culture than a foreign police would be. Secondly, by using local people there is a long-term capacity benefit. These people will return to the Chadian police with a year of modern policing experience.

Complementing and supporting civilian actors

Throughout the preparation of the mission it has been clear that both the EU military and the United Nations have a role as stability providers for the protection of civilians and the populations of the camps. There are armed conflicts between some groups and the government, but we have always made clear that the intention is not to intervene in this internal violent political struggle. It is vital not to be mistakenly seen to be taking sides.

Civilian actors present in the future area of operation have been kept informed about plans since the beginning. In general they welcomed the announcement of a EUFOR military force, and indeed they were among those who drew the attention of the international community to the worsening of the security situation in the first place.

It is unavoidable that there will be anxieties when humanitarian and military actors operate in the same area. We have met local political leaders and have made an effort to involve them too. Above all, patience and coordination are vital during the implementation phase and a good start has already been made.

There is a certain symbiosis between security and development ...

Yes, and that is why we need to work on both tracks simultaneously. This is what we are trying to do in Chad. There will be a convincing military presence and civilian actors working on long-term aspects at the same time. The European Commission has a long-term approach to Chad that will continue. The development work will benefit from the military because it will be less risky to implement projects.

Bahai refugee camp in Chad.

In the long term it is hoped that our development aid will help to improve the living conditions in the country, long after the military leave. It's a good example of how the two tracks can work in parallel and reinforce each other.

Hopes for the future?

Our work together with the United Nations has defined timelines and clear, but limited objectives: that is, to train and pay a stipend to Chadian police officers. Maybe we will continue to work with the United Nations after the initial year.

The preparation work for the elections is more complex. Implementation of the agreement signed by political parties in October 2007 has perhaps been slower than expected. The Commission played a key role in securing the agreement, but its success depends on the will of the local parties to hold elections, and it is not for foreigners to interfere with that.

During the time of the deployment we can expect that the security situation will improve. The force will be strong and well equipped. However, the long-term picture depends largely on the development of the political situation not only in Chad, but also in the wider region. If the problems in Darfur continue, which we hope they will not, there will be an impact on Chad. If the rivalries between the tribes in eastern Chad continue, the security situation will develop accordingly.

The Sudanese in the Darfur region fled the civil war that threatened their homes.
© Alvaro Ybarra Zavala / Agence VU / Chad

A Sudanese refugee at the border between Sudan and Chad.
© Alvaro Ybarra Zavala / Agence VU / Chad

INTERVIEW|**SERGIO SCUERO**
Desk officer for Chad, EC Directorate-General for Development

The background of EU development cooperation with Chad

EU development cooperation with Chad goes back many years to agreements under the Cotonou and Lomé conventions. Chad is a fragile state and through the different cycles of programming, the European Union has invested more than US$ 1 billion in the country.

Between 2000 and 2007, the Ninth European Development Fund (EDF) committed around €228 million to projects in Chad. The EDF strategy for the country for the period 2008 - 2013 has been approved and will have a combined envelope of €311 million. This represents an increase of more than one-third over the previous period.

In the Ninth EDF, the main focuses were infrastructure and water supply, especially considering that Chad is a landlocked country. This was to support progress towards the Millennium Development Goals. This focus continues but additionally includes good governance.

Chad used to have a rural economy based on the 'white gold' of cotton and cattle. The economy changed dramatically in 2004, when oil revenues first came in. The economy is now 80 per cent based on oil revenues. To give that some context, Chad is only the tenth largest exporter of oil on the African continent. Nevertheless, it is still very significant for the country. In 2007, oil revenues amounted to US$ 1 billion.

The work ahead

Over the next few years at least, thanks to the high prices, Chad should continue to gain high revenues from oil, even if production decreases. There is the problem of limited 'absorption capacity', which is the country's ability to use the funds allocated to it. There is also the question of transparency in how oil revenues are used to fight poverty. We should not forget that Chad is one of the poorest countries in the world.

We have a big task ahead on good governance and we must take the political fragility of the situation into account. We need to develop an approach to support Chad in its legislative elections in 2009. The Commission Delegation in N'Djamena plays a role of facilitation between different parties. On 13 August 2007 the government and opposition signed an agreement regarding elections in 2009. Civil society has also become involved. This presents a real window of opportunity to reinforce the rule of law in Chad.

Unfortunately recent clashes in the east have broken the earlier peace agreements with rebels. Our hope is that these agreements can be revived, and that rebel groups will disarm and enter the political arena. We have to ensure that in 2009 there will be a peaceful alternative to the use of arms.

EUFOR will be very useful in meeting immediate needs in the east but it does not have the mandate to provide a sustainable answer. The force will leave after one year so we need an exit strategy. Oil has a part to play in the future and the economy is growing at around 4 per cent a year. However, sustainable development depends on boosting Chad's 'real' economy. Oil does not give an increase in food or employment.

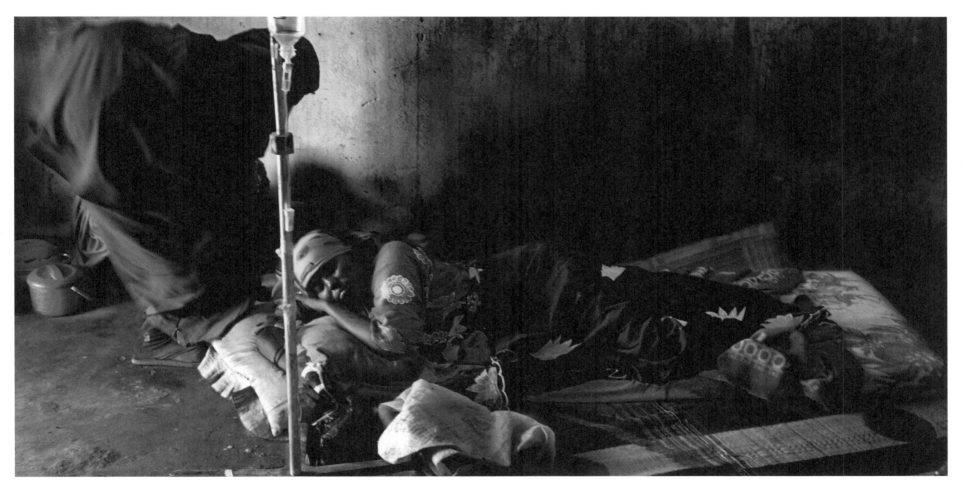

Inside one of the hospitals at the refugee camps.
© Alvaro Ybarra Zavala / Agence VU / Chad

An internally displaced woman in the middle of the desert, near the border with Chad.
© Alvaro Ybarra Zavala / Agence VU / Chad

Chad is in a sensitive region and there are interrelating internal and external factors. To find a solution, you have to solve equations at domestic, regional and international level. There is spillover from Darfur and the Central African Republic to consider, as well as an international picture that includes diverse actors such as Libya, China and Sudan, each with its own interests.

Using oil revenues to development and stability

The World Bank put a mechanism in place to ensure that at least 70 per cent of Chad's oil revenues would be used on priority sectors to combat poverty. When the Chadian government and the World Bank clashed over the rigidity of this agreement, the European Commission played a role as facilitator to resolve the dispute.

Our aim is to reinforce the weak capacity of the government. Part of this challenge is to support the framework to use all revenues — oil and non-oil — in a more transparent way. It will be crucial to support the watchdog that monitors how oil revenue is spent. The Chadian government also needs to commit to the European Transparency Initiative. Follow-up is vital. The international community must speak with one voice to support on the one hand and monitor on the other.

There have been some positive signs. Spending on infrastructure has been encouraging, for example. Progress has been much weaker in the social sectors, however. Little has been invested, partly because of the lack of social policies to back up the spending.

Instead of being negative towards our Chadian partners, we need to support them proactively in the issues they face. We want to encourage them to avoid becoming over-dependent on oil revenues, which are volatile and could fall in future. Wage inflation is a particular associated risk here. The key is to develop and make best use of revenue from other sources.

The visit of Development Commissioner Louis Michel to Chad from 20–22 January 2008 confirms the Commission's ongoing commitment to development cooperation and humanitarian aid, part of the European Union's multi-faceted support to the area.

EU partnerships contributing to a positive change

Even if we are not operating an integrated mission, cooperation between the different EU actors so far has been positive. On the military side, EUFOR will cover the UN work and provide better protection to refugees and displaced people. This will also create a better environment for humanitarian efforts.

At the same time, we realise the military aspect is a spot action and has limited duration. That is why we are launching a Linking Relief, Rehabilitation and Development (LRRD) process. The European Commission is targeting eastern Chad and Central Africa with a package of €13 million providing schools, hospitals and drinking water. This makes the link between humanitarian relief and rehabilitation, and allows development actions to take place as soon as security is established.

The €311 million EDF package will ensure durability to these actions, with the emphasis on good governance, the 'real' economy and water supplies. This means that we have a package that offers action in the short term and durability in the medium term.

61

The Chadian refugee camps are filled with war widows and ophans.
© Alvaro Ybarra Zavala
Agence VU
Chad

All these different efforts are complementary to each other — from the European Commission's support, through the Instrument for Stability, to the UN MINURCAT mission. The financial support for training and deploying Chadian police forces will help increase security in camps for refugees and IDPs.

Our strategy is over five years. We can't talk longer term than that because the situation is so multi-layered and volatile. In Chad, we still have an open crisis and we have to see what happens on the ground in the coming months. In the medium term we hope that political dialogue will lead to credible and transparent elections in 2009.

If the situation stabilises, we will have the opportunity to make progress on good governance. We hope the development agenda will reduce poverty and bring a peace dividend. This is crucial. If the economy weakens in the years ahead and the political and development roadmaps are not on track, then undesirable scenarios can open up.

The Instrument for Stability gives flexibility and time

It is more flexible than the Rapid Reaction Mechanism, which was limited to actions of six months. It also allows greater flexibility in our procedures to implement EDF funds, for example in emergency situations. The procedures have been simplified and accelerated.

It is important to note that you cannot always easily classify in terms of humanitarian aid and development aid. There are grey zones and you need to have a strategy that accounts for that.

Of course, funding can make a difference but the money must be well spent, with the right coordination and the right political approach behind it. Chad has oil revenues of US$ 1 billion a year, so an EU development contribution of around €300 million over five years will not gain leverage in itself. Making a difference requires all the instruments to be used together. Only then can we gain the critical mass necessary to help stabilise the sub-region.

INTERVIEW | **THIERRY BOUCHER**
| **Deputy Administrator, Athena[3]**

Providing security and protection

The context of the planned military operation in eastern Chad is one of ongoing crisis in neighbouring Darfur. In eastern Chad, refugees from Darfur as well as internally displaced persons in camps are in the need of security, both to improve their lives in camps and as a precondition for the return of displaced persons to a normal life in their regions of origin. Since the United Nations is deploying a peace-keeping operation in Darfur, our aim is to do something for eastern Chad.

The EUFOR mandate is to protect the UN staff when the trained Chadian police are deployed in the refugee camps. There will be a review after six months; it will also have to be seen whether a UN deployment of troops would be useful or not.

The Chadian government preferred a EU military presence to UN troops. This is because of the complex political situation in Chad, a country that has historically been subject to dispute and influence from France and Libya in particular. It was understood that a EUFOR force would be largely French. Since France has maintained a presence including some armed elements in Chad since 1983, the force can act as a continuation. It can also avoid a politically sensitive change in the composition or balance of the international presence.

Links between the European Union's military and civil operations

The EU treaty provides that expenditure on military operations may not be financed from the budget of European communities, only through Member States' contributions. The EU budget may not finance common civilian-military missions, and the European Commission – or any instrument operated by it – can only finance what are termed 'accompanying measures' in this context.

We have two parallel tracks. The Council manages the military operation itself. There may be cooperation in theatre, however. For example the force and the EC delegation could run projects that both help the population and give some positive visibility to the EU force. These kinds of actions can help the local population to understand that the military is there to help them, and is not acting as an occupying force of some kind.

Every military operation conducted by the European Union includes a communication policy. In the mission in the Democratic Republic of Congo, for example, there were radio spots and a newsletter to help the local population understand the nature and purpose of the work being done.

The aim is to help stabilise eastern Chad. Troops can of course provide security in the short term, but helping internally displaced persons return home is what will provide stability in the long run.

3   Mechanism to administer the common costs of EU operations having military or defence implications, established by Council Decision 2007/384/CFSP.

64

A refugee convoy taking
people to the Bahai
refugee camp.
© Alvaro Ybarra Zavala
Agence VU / Chad

DEMOCRATIC REPUBLIC OF THE CONGO

Support of the security system reform

REPORTAGE BY PATRICIA MCCRACKEN

PHOTOGRAPHS & CAPTIONS BY MARCUS BLEADSDALE

Soldiers control crowds along Kinshasa's streets whenever the heavily armed presidential convoy passes, sometimes three times daily. Streets are closed down and movement is restricted.
© Marcus Bleasdale / Agence VII / From the book: *One Hundred Years of Darkness - A Photographic Journey into the Heart of Congo*, by Jon Swain and Marcus Bleasdale, 2002

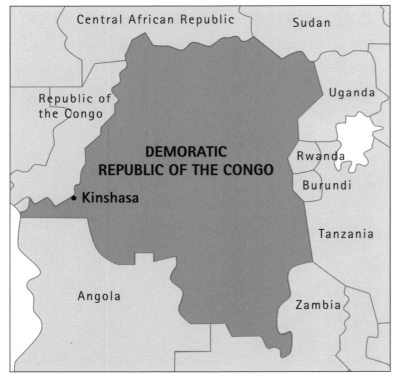

Central African Republic

Sudan

Republic of
the Congo

Uganda

**DEMORATIC
REPUBLIC OF THE CONGO**

Rwanda

Burundi

• **Kinshasa**

Tanzania

Angola

Zambia

© GOPA-Cartermill

Capital: Kinshasa

Area: 2,344,858 km²

Population: 62,636,000 (2007)

Life expectancy at birth: male 44.3 years; female 47.0 years (2005)

Government type: unitary multiparty republic with two legislative bodies

GNI – per capita: US$ 128 (2006)

Source: © 2008 Encyclopædia Britannica, Inc.

INTRODUCTION

The hole that is dug into the ground is wide enough to fit the body of a man into it, but just barely. A man will shimmy down into the snug hole, carrying with him makeshift tools, which he uses to loosen the diamonds which are embedded in the unstable walls of earth that engulf him.

Extracting natural treasures from the dirt in the Democratic Republic of Congo (DRC) is a life-threatening job destined for men of no means; the diamonds collected will be sold for a song to fuel the bloodletting that has raged for decades on the ground above.

The DRC is a land enriched with precious minerals, bountiful rain forests and an abundance of natural resources. It is vast, about the size of Western Europe, and has been the stage for extreme brutality, massacres, multiple wars and the depths of poverty for more than a hundred years. The Congo is a lesson in the consequence of exploitation, maintaining a legacy of corruption rooted deeper than the diamonds themselves.

One of the most notorious rulers to overtly devastate this country was Belgian King Leopold II, who, in the 1800s, brutally took advantage of what was then a Belgian colony, leaving much to ruin. Since then it has been a cat's paw in the cold war, and had its leader assassinated and replaced by a thieving dictator, Mobutu, who inspired the word 'kleptocracy'. Mobutu changed his name to Mobutu Sese Seko, changed the name of the country to Zaire, and robbed and plundered his way through 30 years of

Women from a makeshift camp for displaced refugees in Goma. They are often raped by government soldiers in these woods. There have been 30,000 reported rapes in the DRC per year in the past four years. The actual number is thought to be four times that.
© Marcus Bleasdale / Agence VII / Congo

A makeshift camp for displaced refugees in Goma.
They fled the fighting between government forces and
General Nkunda in Karuba and Mushake, Kivu Province.
© Marcus Bleasdale / Agence VII / Congo

dictatorship. He was finally pushed into exile after civil war erupted when the 1994 genocide in neighboring Rwanda spilled over into DRC. Yet another long and devastating civil war, and another assassination of a leader, brings us to the convoluted mayhem that is today's Congo.

President Joseph Kabila became Africa's youngest head of state at the age of 29, having taken over the office when his father was assassinated in 2001. Two years ago, elections were held and Kabila was democratically voted into office.

A peace accord in 2003 to settle the second civil war called for the creation of a new national army to be drawn from the mix of armed groups that had formed over the years. But the army is fledgling, at best, with divided allegiances among its ranks and only corruption in common. It is an army which, to a large extent, derides the practice of human rights, or even humanity itself. It is an army that murders, rapes and tortures with alarming regularity, often aiming its persecution at opponents of Kabila.

As fighting continues to flare up, there is no let-up in the misery of the people forced to flee. Many internally displaced persons from previous rounds of combat dare not return to their homes, and their numbers are swelled by newcomers seeking a safe haven.

The nation sees more than 1,200 people die each day as a result of fighting and chaos. Life expectancy is 47.2 years. And maybe most telling of all, the United Nation's largest peace-keeping mission is stationed in DRC.

Government soldiers relax after winning their first battle in months
against General Nkunda in Karuba, Kivu Province.
© Marcus Bleasdale / Agence VII / Congo

PROJECT FACTS & FIGURES

Programme
Installation of an integrated system of
human resources management for the
future Congolese Police

Location
Democratic Republic of Congo

Total amount sponsored by IfS
€5,000,000

Project start
February 2008

Duration
18 months

Partners
Complementary with actions
undertaken by the European Union

Target group
Congolese police services

THE DRC AND THE EUROPEAN UNION

The UN Organisation Mission in DRC (MONUC) and others, such as the ESDP mission and European Communications Security & Evaluation Agency of the Military Committee (EUSEC) have initiated programmes in the defence sector which have resulted in slight improvements in training, living conditions, pay, chain of command and prosecution for those accused of crimes. And it appears that abuses in the army have, as a result, declined in recent months. But security can only improve if those efforts are carried out in both the police and the justice sector.

The DRC police are a ragbag of various other security forces, made up mostly of amateurs, ex-gendarme, ex-civil guard and ex-militia (even Mai-Mai, a rebel group, who believe that rubbing themselves with oil and taking antibiotics makes them bullet-proof). The Congolese police are severely undertrained, underpaid, understaffed, and without proper weapons or uniforms.

It is unclear exactly how many police there are in the country, but a head-count and control of the pay roll puts the number

A makeshift camp for displaced refugees in Goma.
They fled the fighting between government forces and
General Nkunda in Karuba and Mushake, Kivu Province.
© Marcus Bleasdale / Agence VII / Congo

at 103,807, a service which is expected to serve and protect a population of some 65 million. And the current state of the police service is one which, despite some definite improvement, still bribes, bullies, robs and torments the people it is in place to assist and sanction. It is a service without a formal chain of command, and without a doubt, a detriment to society in its current form.

Under the Instrument for Stability (IfS), €5million has been allocated to aid the Congolese in building a police service that can protect its citizens, not threaten them: one that can restore and maintain order, and can encourage and support a stable internal security; which will, in turn, support a stable democracy.

The primary objective of the project is the creation of an integrated system of human resource management, which will allow a functioning police service to survive and sustain within Congo's troubled borders. The project will hire staff to organize change, perform much-needed analyses, and create basic infrastructure to a civil function that does not yet exist in the DRC.

General Ngodjolo's men in Zumbe outside Bunia.
© Marcus Bleasdale / Agence VII / Congo

PROJECT OBJECTIVES

The objective, an integrated system of human resources management (HRM) for the future Congolese Police, is the first step of the overall police reform which is as unquestionable as the reform of the army.

Background

The police service in DRC does not, in general, exist. It is a combination of ex-militia, ex-gendarme, ex-civil guard and amateurs that loosely operate throughout the country. They are an underpaid, understaffed group that works without sufficient management, direction or structure. Thus, instead of protecting and sanctioning the public, many acting as police officers abuse civilians.

Specific objectives

To get the national police service ready for the reforms following actions will be taken:

- financing of a technical assistant at the level of the executive secretariat of the committee that follows up on the police reform (an expert profile programme manager, a specialist in organisational change and two others who will multitask)

- specific technical assistance to the Secretariat of the Committee on Police Reform for the installation of an integrated HRM system (two or three experts in profiling and in developing needs functions)

- financing the creation of the action plan for collective information

- financing the needs of the human resources management at the level of the general commissary:
  - infrastructure
  - informatics equipment
  - furniture
  - selection and purchase of software for human resource management.

A makeshift camp for displaced refugees in Goma.
They fled the fighting between government forces and
General Nkunda in Karuba and Mushake, Kivu Province.
© Marcus Bleasdale / Agence VII / Congo

INTERVIEW | **JOAQUIM SALGUEIRO**
International Relations Officer for DRC, EC
Directorate-General for External Relations

The scope of the problem

Talking about DRC, you need to first of all imagine a country of about 65 million inhabitants, the size of Western Europe, without infrastructures, having suffered from 30 years of dictatorship and recently six years of civil war. Since 2002, peace has been almost restored throughout the country, but state authority has basically been absent for at least the last 15 years.

This obviously has had consequences on the police, which still lacks the resources to function, but also a proper command structure, and even police staff – we don't know how many there are – do not have a clear idea of their mission and responsibilities.

The police administration needs to be reformed and modernised in order to match the resources (human, financial and technical) of the sector with the needs of the population. This reform work has to be carried out within all the structures (from the local police stations to the Ministry of Interior), starting from a top-down approach, but based on multi-disciplinary inputs from field police officers (Congolese, African, international), administrators, citizens and civil society organisations.

While we are aware of all the constraints impeding the police from functioning adequately, one of the main frustrations is that some police officers, instead of systematically protecting the population and defending the rule of law, often abuse people, financially and physically, thus damaging the image of the function.

Moving from lawless to lawful: a tall order

The need for reform of the police is enshrined in a wider context of insecurity and impunity, itself the result of decades of bad governance and dismissal of the state authority.

Like most other sectors, one of the consequences of these large-scale problems is the fact that security officers are generally not paid, or very minimally, and they may use their uniform or function to 'help themselves' from the population, resulting in a very poor image of the police. Moreover, the role and mission of security officers has gradually become unclear to both themselves and the population, so there tends to be a chaotic situation, as people no longer trust the police, and consider it is up to people to defend and protect themselves.

Changing these habits and mentality where everyone cares for themselves, and restoring acceptance and trust in the police officer, both as the one who protects and as the one who may sanction, will be time and cost-consuming, but is essential for the good functioning of the state.

After almost ten years of war, and the absence for even longer of public means and of an effective administration, the situation of the police had become quite chaotic. The GMRR (Groupe Mixte de Réflexion sur la Réforme et la Réorganisation de la Police Nationale Congolaise) study carried out in 2006 outlined that the current police was the result of a mix of professional, unprofessional, military and civilian, young and should-be retired officers, thus requiring a comprehensive reform and reorganisation.

President Joseph Kabila faces a statue of independence hero Patrice Lumumba, who was assassinated barely six months after the 'official' end of colonial rule.
© Marcus Bleasdale / Agence VII / From the book: One hundred Years of Darkness - A Photographic Journey into the heart of Congo, by Jon Swain and Marcus Bleasdale, 2002

Under the watchful eye of the military,
a crowd 'greets' President Joseph Kabila. People are organised and
transported to public events in support of their leader.

© Marcus Bleasdale / Agence VII / From the book: One Hundred Years
of Darkness - A Photographic Journey into the Heart of Congo, by
Jon Swain and Marcus Bleasdale, 2002

Where to start: revamp human resources

Most of the recommendations the report put forward concerned the need for restructuring and upgrading the human resources (HR) component, so as to gradually build a modern and efficient police, adequately trained and paid to respond to the needs of the population, and understanding their role in promoting the rule of law and protecting the population.

The qualitative upgrade thus consists in reorganising the different police services falling under the authority of the Ministry of Interior and devising a real HR policy, based on a better correlation between what is expected from the police and the means at their disposal (in terms of staff, but also training, equipment, regulations/legislation, etc.) so that police officers can carry out their tasks in the most effective and responsible manner.

One of the first actions of that wide human resources reform is the launching of a census (financed by the European Commission), both quantitative (assessing the number of police officers in service) and qualitative (identifying their needs, training received, grade, past and current responsibilities). The information received from this 'mapping' should enable the Congolese police authorities to better allocate their resources in line with the HR situation and requirements of the police. This exercise is supported with a reorganisation of the management for human resources and training of the staff. In addition they have been reallocated to an administration building sitting together with budget and finance management and the National Congolese Police IT services. This would then enable the police to better manage its human resources, training and any other activities.

Repairing what is broken

The HR situation is completely unclear: we do not know how many police officers there are (figures oscillate between 75,000 and 115,000), their age,

their training (although it is known that there has not been any structured training in the past ten years), their background (civilian/military), how they have been recruited, their grade. Most of the police officers are unpaid or very low paid, not fed and unhealthy.

In most provinces, there are no police station premises, in Kinshasa itself police stations are simple containers; arms are available in profusion throughout the country, but the police have very few; there is almost no possibility of communication, and there are almost no vehicles (and fuel) available. But thanks to the support programme for the elections, one in five police officers may now have a uniform.

Signs of promise

The reform of the police sector has to be seen in a wider context of constraints which the country has to face: notably, a heritage of years of bad governance, absence of structural reforms for over a decade, malfunctioning or almost nonexistent administration, very limited public finances and rampant impunity.

Work towards reforming the sector has started during the transition, but being at the core of the state sovereignty, it is one of the most difficult sectors in which to advocate and bring about change. Hence, it is significantly positive that the authorities and key police managers and decision makers are now supporting the reform, and gradually owning some of its key elements (such as the governance contract) as they see the potential benefits of the adjustments planned.

The past months have showed that despite insufficient funds and difficult working conditions, improvements are possible and people are increasingly embracing favourable and constructive stances.

Refugees who fled fighting in Gbadolite 1999–2000, pitch camp on a sandbar between Congo and the Central African Republic. The town of Gbadolite, site of former Zairean dictator Mobutu Sese Seko's lavish palace, was destroyed by fighting and is now home to Jean Pierre Bemba's Ugandan-backed rebel movement.

© Marcus Bleasdale / Agence VII / From the book: One Hundred Years of Darkness – A Photographic Journey into the Heart of Congo, by Jon Swain and Marcus Bleasdale, 2002

Gety, Ituri District
A religious service takes place in the early morning
at the Gety camp for internally displaced persons.
© Marcus Bleasdale / Agence VII / From the book: One Hundred Years of
Darkness - A Photographic Journey into the Heart of Congo, by Jon Swain and
Marcus Bleasdale, 2002

A concrete positive result has been the creation of an integrated police unit, some 1,000 police officers operating in Kinshasa, fully trained, with the mission to protect the country's institutions and personnel in the transition period. A rapid protection unit of some 3,500 officers, preventing riots, has contributed to reestablish public order in Kinshasa.

Trust as a bridge

Thanks to very close and continuous dedication to personal relations, trust has been built between the EC Delegation and persons in charge within the Inspectorate General, the Ministry of the Interior as well as civil society. These all agree with the approach suggested and the necessity of a police reform based upon demilitarisation and establishing a real public service. Even though it has taken several months to get a prime ministerial decree allowing for the creation of the CSRP (Comité de Suivi de la Réforme de la Police) to be signed, resilience, trust building and persuasiveness have borne fruit to the satisfaction of all partners, Congolese and international.

A country with huge potential

We need to keep in mind where the country comes from. We need to acknowledge the substantial progress made since 2002: a peace agreement, a peaceful transition which led to elections, an elected president and elected multipartite national and provincial assembly, a balanced budget – even if very small in light of the needs of the country, a relevant and ambitious government programme and an agenda for governance reforms.

The DRC is a country with serious difficulties that impede progress, but with such a huge potential, with a young and willing population striving for peace and prosperity.

Change (regarding the mentality, habits, working methods) will not come about within a day, and we should not expect it to. Reforms take time and require a strong political will for forcing through good governance reforms, which is a very difficult challenge in a nascent democracy where the population has huge expectations.

The main difficulty in a post-conflict country like the DRC is that every single progress depends to some extent on several others, and each sector (health, education, justice, police, agriculture, infrastructure, etc.) needs reforming and funds for it.

A makeshift camp for displaced refugees in Goma. They fled the fighting
between government forces and General Nkunda in Karuba and Mushake, Kivu Province.
© Marcus Bleasdale / Agence VII / Congo

INTERVIEW | LEILA BOUCHEBOUBA
| **Task manager, EC Delegation to the DRC**

Starting from scratch

There is no such thing as a police force here. We have in DRC a mix of everything that has been put together since 1997, following the [2002 peace] agreement up to recent years. Even if it is a bit different than for the army, the police service (and not force) has a bit more than 100,000 agents: ex-gendarmes, ex-civil guard, ex-military, ex-militia – so a bit of everything, coming from the last decade of conflict. Moreover, the police have never been seen as what we can consider as a public service. From the military police of the colonial time, to the police forces with military status from the Mobutu era, police agents and the population do not know how to behave with each other.

The question is not only to modernise and reorganise the service. It is really to support the democratisation process in helping the government and the president (as security is a shared competence) in the redefinition of the national security policy within a democracy, if possible, in peace with its neighbouring countries. In doing that, the police service will only focus on the security of citizens and their belongings as well as ensure public order. And that is what we are aiming at in supporting the police reform.

A makeshift camp for displaced refugees in Goma. They fled the fighting between government forces and General Nkunda in Karuba and Mushake, Kivu Province.
© Marcus Bleasdale / Agence VII / Congo

Gety, Ituri District, July 2006.
A UN vehicle unit and the UN-APC, drive down a road near Gety. Congo DRC held its first democratic election in 46 years on 30 July 2006. The elections were supported by the international community who also deployed a UN peace keeping operation to maintain security during the election period.
© Marcus Bleasdale / Agence VII / Congo

A key problem

Police agents aren't always policing, but are often being used as private guards, cleaning in front of houses or carrying the bags of women doing their shopping. This is the negation of a public service; those who can afford it have the right to security. Moreover this is creating discrepancies within the institution and the police agents: those that are deployed to private operators are fed and are generating funds, while the ones left over are not fed and are not generating funds. This makes it very tempting for commanders to 'create' new police agents by giving them a uniform and then sending this 'new' recruit on private missions to earn more money.

The gap in society in the perception of the police service is well illustrated by the fact that people don't find it shocking to see police agents available 24 hours a day doing everything and nothing. Therefore as long as individuals within the institution are treated the way they are, there is not going to be any improvement. This is not only a question of training and professionalism.

Police agents have to realise that, like all of us, they have rights. The way they are mistreated nowadays, the lack of working conditions, of social conditions, of appropriate equipment, of proper training and moreover lack of basic human consideration, are reasons, but not excuses to act inappropriately towards the population. And the population itself is not used to having the opportunity to speak up when security is in question. This is the very important point of the reform, to let people understand that we are all of concern: the citizen, the state and the public services.

And that it is especially because of our rights; that we define common rules via our legislators, and that public state services, such as the police, are the ones in charge to make sure we all respect them. And while doing so they have means, including the use of force, in order to protect citizens and to maintain public order.

The project initiated under the IfS and which is followed up by FED activities, as well as activities implemented by an ESDP police mission, is part of this overall reform. It is the first and necessary step towards a new police service. This project is ambitious as it is attacking the core of illegal fund generation, it is a logistical challenge, and it is a really new way of thinking in an institution where human resources are neglected.

Working together

Working with our counterparts is challenging, since you get excited and depressed on the very same day. In this particular sector of intervention you need to get into the institution and try to understand all the functioning of the system, as even if it seems to be chaotic, there is a kind of organisation. Most interestingly, you get in touch with all ranks in the institution and you feel that there is a tremendous potential: debate around the code of conduct, the will to get training, the need to question, discuss and ask about the reform – all of this is really fundamental as the reform will only be possible if all the Congolese partners feel involved.

That is why the civil society has to play an important role to lobby, to really put on the top of the political agenda the question of interior security. With them, as well, response and cooperation is of good quality and trust is essential.

At the level of the Minister of the Interior and the highest rank of the police you start to feel that some are 100 per cent supporting the demilitarisation – the police service and not police forces – and the idea of serving the population and not controlling citizens. Moreover, due to the fact that we are focusing on central services, it is sometimes frustrating for our counterparts, who would like rapid results, especially in the operational field. But there is some sign from the police project team and its work. The head of the police has already realised that he needs an administration, and he has decided, which was a surprise to a lot of the traditional bilateral cooperation in this sector, to send around 500 police agents for training.

The role of the European Commission, not being a classical bilateral partner in the police sector, is giving us an added value. We try to work on institutional development; we try to bring something different and not to come with the same background as police officers. Because we are civilians we are not inhibited by a hierarchy and we can exchange ideas more freely and challenge high-ranking officers. Therefore the partnership between the European Commission and the Congolese National Police is different and based on a solid level of trust.

But this trust has to be demonstrated all the time. It is a permanent struggle, as our intervention is focusing on the sustainability of the results, while often the intervention in this sector is focused on quick wins and not pushing Congolese police officers or Congolese Interior Ministry civil servants to develop their own competence.

So it is important to always say the truth, explain what is possible and what is not possible, and to stick clearly to principles. This is the only way a certain understanding and cooperation can exist.

Friends and family attend the funeral of Mapenzi Boloma, a 10 month-old girl, who died of diarrhoea and vomiting in the village of Gety, Ituri District, 17 July 2006. She died just a few days after arriving to the camp, together with 18 other people who died on the same day, merely days before the historic elections in the DRC. Ongoing conflict and the lack of access to medical care have claimed the lives of four million people in the DRC since 1998.

© Marcus Bleasdale / Agence VII / Congo

A child soldier rides back to his base in Ituri Province, Eastern Congo.
© Marcus Bleasdale / Agence VII / Congo

GUINEA BISSAU

Security sector reform and combating drugs

REPORTAGE BY DANIELA SCHRÖDER

PHOTOGRAPHS & CAPTIONS BY REBECCA BLACKWELL & JUSTIN SUTCLIFFE

Sekou Tidiane Bangoura, arrested for theft, peers through the bars
of a cell housing 14 men at the judicial police headquarters in Bissau, Guinea Bissau.
© Rebecca Blackwell / AP Photo / Guinea Bissau

© GOPA-Cartermill

Capital: Bissau

Area: 36,125 km²

Population: 1,472,000 (2007)

Life expectancy at birth: male 44.8 years; female 48.5 years

Government type: republic with one legislative house

Note: Legal ambiguity persists in November 2007. A constitution adopted by the National Assembly in 2001 has been neither promulgated nor vetoed by the President

GNI – per capita: US$ 186 (2006)

Source: © 2008 Encyclopædia Britannica, Inc.

A sports-utility vehicle, one of many in the capital, drives past decaying colonial buildings and a market stall selling nuts in central Bissau. According to police there are several Hummers in the capital — a car worth more than 100 times the average annual salary. Some of the owners are unemployed men in their 20s–30s.
© Rebecca Blackwell / AP Photo / Guinea Bissau

INTRODUCTION

Once considered a potential model for sustainable development on the African continent, Guinea Bissau is now one of the five poorest countries in the world. The recent civil war caused substantial damage to the country's finances and infrastructure and set back much of the progress that had already been made. Since the war an indecisive government has led to further low growth in 2002–2006. As a result the tiny nation on Africa's west coast faces inequality of income distribution as well as deep-rooted security and justice challenges.

Guinea Bissau won its independence in 1974 after a protracted liberation war that resulted in the dislocation of about one-fifth of the population and the destruction of important economic infrastructure. For several years the country was governed by a revolutionary council. The first multi-party election was held in 1994 but democracy was soon overshadowed by the outbreak of a civil war. This worsened the climate of political instability, insecurity and underdevelopment.

Today, although relatively calm, this small African country, which is off most people's radar screens, still struggles with the prevalence of political instability, divisions in society and destruction of social and economic infrastructure. This situation is worsened by a high degree of corruption and more recently also the impact of organised crime, especially the flourishing drugs trade from South America.

Guinea Bissau's Prime Minister, Martinho Dafa Cabi, says that the international community
should do more to help fight drug trafficking here. Cocaine use, he points out, is a mainly Western problem.
© Justin Sutcliffe / The Sunday Telegraph 2007 / Guinea Bissau

Guinea Bissau is considered to be one of Africa's major drugs transit hubs. International drugs experts fear the poor country with its numerous, uninhibited islands could become a 'narco-state'. The value of cocaine trafficked through Guinea Bissau is estimated to be higher than the entire national income.

Every year an estimated 40 tonnes of pure Colombian cocaine is supposedly in transit through the mainland's mangrove swamps and the chain of islands that make up the country. Most of it goes to the lucrative markets in Europe. One of the most serious impediments for fighting serious crime is that Guinea Bissau has few or no resources for the justice system and in addition no proper prisons since the only jail was destroyed in the civil war. The country's network of tidal creeks coupled with a fragile economic situation and justice system means that drugs smugglers can operate with impunity. The prospect of making big money with relatively few risks lures many young businesspeople into the drugs trade. Western intelligence sources admit that so far they have underestimated the scale of the problem, but they now consider Guinea Bissau as the most serious drugs trafficking case on the African continent.

Apart from the roaring drugs business, the country's macroeconomic situation is serious and gives few signs for hope. However efforts of the World Bank and the IMF are slowly reinstating the trust of the international community. Guinea Bissau's economy is based primarily on farming and fishing activities, representing about 63 per cent of gross domestic product (GDP). Agriculture generates 80 per cent of livelihoods and 90 per cent of exports, primarily through unprocessed cashew nuts.

Cashews aside, Guinea Bissau has few natural resources. The vital crop is the country's principal source of legitimate income and the main source of foreign exchange, followed by fishing exports.

Per capita growth has in recent years dropped (from US$ 900 in 2006 to US$ 600 in 2007) and approximately 80 per cent of the population lives on less than US$ 2 per day with 16 per cent existing in extreme poverty on less than US$ 1 per day.

Some 60 per cent of its meagre state budget is financed by foreign aid. However, much of this has to be spent on foreign debt payments. External debt is equal to at least three times GDP or around ten times annual export earnings.

Renovation of the basic infrastructure damaged during the 1998–1999 fighting has barely begun. It makes the engagement of international agencies committed to involvement in the reconstruction process more complicated. In addition, the fragile political situation scares away potential investors.

Guinea Bissau has struggled to restore stable civilian rule following the military coup of September 2003 and legislative and presidential elections of March 2004 and June–July 2005, respectively. Governance is currently obstructed by fighting political factions and there is a prevailing risk of another breakdown of existing political arrangements before the next legislative elections. The polls were originally due in early 2008 but have been postponed until end 2008 with a possibility of delaying until 2009 to coincide with the presidential elections.

The country's armed forces are seen as the greatest threat to the stabilisation of the weak political institutions. Following its victory over the Portuguese, the military became the dominant and most legitimate political power in Guinea Bissau. The armed forces continue to exert enormous influence over the country's political life, despite the civilian transition of 2003–2005 and a concurrent process of demobilisation.

Large relative to the size and resources of the country, the military forces have traditionally refused to countenance a reduction in their size and power, while complaining of the government's inability to finance them in peacetime. The choice has been either to drain already scarce state resources or to face military revolt. With the recruitment of thousands of new militia in the 1998–1999 conflict, the situation was exacerbated beyond the control of civilian governance.

As is the case with other countries emerging from years of violent conflict, a specific problem in Guinea Bissau is to reintegrate veterans of war into society. Since previous reintegration efforts by the international community have been less successful, some veterans of the war of independence have remobilised.

In addition, family members of the veterans of the colonial liberalisation war claim financial compensation while the legal rules on who qualifies for reintegration support remain unclear.

According to government figures, around 6,500 veterans from both wars are to be demobilised. There are also 8,000 to 9,000 soldiers still serving who expect to be demobilised or to retire in planned future efforts. The aim is to downsize the numbers to a total of 3,000 in the armed forces.

Guinea Bissau's scarce financial resources and the weakness of its state institutions make it difficult for the country to address the numerous difficulties and move forward with the much-needed reforms. The key challenges for the country in the period ahead will be to restore fiscal discipline, rebuild public administration, improve the climate for private investment and promote economic diversification.

International support is vital for Guinea Bissau's economic and political development. Outside Africa, cooperative relations are focused on Portuguese-speaking countries, most notably Portugal and Brazil, but also on Spain and France.

In addition to international reform efforts led by the European Commission and the United Nations, the Economic Community of West African States (ECOWAS) also plays an important role in making Guinea Bissau more stable and secure. So far its main focus has been in the area of small arms and light weapons and the training of soldiers for peace-keeping activities.

People gather around a speedboat of the type believed to be used by drug traffickers. Guinea Bissau, with its many water ways, is fast becoming a major route for drugs smuggling.
© Rebecca Blackwell / AP Photo / Guinea Bissau

Programme
Technical Assistance in support of
security sector reform (SSR) in Guinea
Bissau

Location
Guinea Bissau

Total eligible costs of the action
European support for the country
will continue to be given through the
Ninth European Development Fund
(EDF). The European Commission has
allocated €7.7 million to disarmament,
demobilisation and reintegration
(DDR) and security sector reform (SSR)
in Guinea Bissau and an additional
€12.5 million to justice and public
administration under the Ninth EDF.
For justice and parliamentary reform,
the Ninth EDF will provide €6 million
for capacity building of the legislature
and the judiciary (PAOSED Programme)

Amount sponsored by IfS
€700,000

Project start
October 2007

Duration
12 months

ACHIEVING SECURITY REFORM AND COMBATING DRUGS

The European Commission has already provided support to
Guinea Bissau under the Eighth European Development Fund
(EDF) for disarmament, demobilisation and reintegration (DDR)
of former combatants and for public sector reform. The European
Commission is also financing support programmes aimed at
pushing justice sector and public administration reforms. A
national security strategy drafted in 2006 provides the country
with an initial framework for a security sector reform (SSR),
focusing mainly on defence issues. However, it also covers some
aspects of justice reform, police and border management.

European support for the country on SSR related matters will
continue to be given through the Ninth EDF and the Tenth EDF. But
the legacy of war, the risk of renewed violence and the impact of
drugs trafficking as well as increasing numbers of illegal migrants
on the way to Europe, made it necessary for the European Union
to provide rapid support. Therefore, the Commission decided to
fund urgent action in Guinea Bissau under the Instrument for
Stability (IfS). The project started in October 2007. It is expected to
cover a period of 12 months until the new EDF starts, but can be
extended if necessary. The Commission aims to coordinate closely
its activities under the IfS with the United Nations and ECOWAS
to ensure complementarity.

The police resources are limited. They only have one computer and their radios are in desperate need of repairs. Officers have to fill reports on old typewriters and there is never enough money to fuel all their vehicles. A recent drugs bust ended with a car chase and most of the drug traffickers escaped as the police ran out of petrol.
It is not incompetence - merely a lack of basic resources.

PROJECT OBJECTIVES

To support the government of Guinea Bissau in implementing its national strategy to reform the security sector.

Specific objectives

- Providing technical assistance through a team of three experts to support the government of Guinea Bissau in implementing its national strategy to reform the security sector.

- Preparing the ground for major EDF and possible other donors' activities in the near future.

- Assisting the government in the demobilisation and reintegration of former war combatants. This action will focus on support to draw up a legal framework for the reform process and to complete remaining censuses.

- Advising the government on the integration of surplus security staff into the private sector and helping to draw up schemes for the retirement of these personnel.

- The overall objective is to help stabilise the political and economic situation in order to push the country's socioeconomic development.

Navy Seal Mohamed Camara Tawal stands on a street corner in central Bissau.
Guinea Bissau currently has an over-dimensioned defence force.
Downsizing the military is part of the country's urgent security sector reform needs.
© Rebecca Blackwell / AP Photo / Guinea Bissau

INTERVIEW | **INGER BUXTON**
Coordinator of the Instrument for Stability SSR support in Guinea Bissau, EC Directorate-General for External Relations

The EU's role in Guinea Bissau

The European Commission has been engaged in Guinea Bissau for many years, but following the civil war at the end of the 1990s the post-conflict peace-building aspects have become more important in our support. The European Union has been involved through the Eight EDF in support of DDR activities.

The DDR process proved to be difficult, in particular when it came to sustainable reintegration of former combatants. Both wars left a number of former military personnel who needed to be demobilised and reintegrated. Still today, there are many ex-soldiers and their families who never received any compensation after the war of independence in the 1970s.

Problems downsizing the military

Thus, many people claim the right to compensation for serving in the military, during the war of independence, and during the civil war in the late 1990s. In addition, Guinea Bissau currently has an over-dimensional defence force. Downsizing the military is part of the urgent SSR needs of the country.

Guinea Bissau is a very fragile country with long-term problems both in terms of political crisis but also in terms of socioeconomic developments. The World Bank has only recently started to re-engage in Guinea Bissau after a political agreement in April 2007, and the international community has begun to restart budget support. However, the number of big donors is limited as many who left are not likely to engage again.

Dealing with problems in a coherent manner

In addition to this, in the last few years the drugs trafficking has increased. The drugs problem is closely linked with reforms in the security sector. If you deal with trafficking it is about border management issues, it is about the sovereignty of the territory of the state, about its ability to protect and monitor the territory. But even if the drugs problem mainly has to do with trafficking, there is also an increasing problem within the country itself. There are signs of an emerging drug use in the country and with drugs cartels present on the ground, the drug trade is also becoming an issue about a functioning justice system and about a police force which has the capacity to deal with these problems.

As these drugs to a great extent end up in Europe, the European Union's political interest in supporting SSR in Guinea Bissau has grown.

Disarmament can only take place when you know what structures and capacities you need in the security forces, when you know who to keep and who to get rid of. Therefore, SSR was identified as one of the priority areas for the EU.

Implementing new security concepts

European countries started showing an increasing interest in SSR in 2006 and early 2007, in particular Portugal, as the incoming EU presidency and the United Kingdom having given advice to the Guinea Bissau on how to develop a national security strategy. With the political commitment to carry out reforms in the security sector, the strategy helped to start a national reform process and provided a framework for reforms. The United Kingdom wanted the European Union to follow up on this since it is not a strong actor in Guinea Bissau.

Furthermore, Guinea Bissau is an interesting case for implementing a new and comprehensive EU approach to SSR which is based on a broad security concept. Security is not only about external threats to the territory of the state and to the interests of the state. Many people do not see external threats as the main threat to themselves. It is the internal threat, the lack of rule of law, the lack of respect for human rights, the lack of access to justice or the fact that the police and the military forces are not able or willing to protect them against physical threats.

There is no point in having a functioning police or justice system without also having functioning prisons and border management facilities, as well as effective democratic and civilian control of the security sector. With the adoption of an overarching EU policy framework in June 2006 the EU has started taking a more holistic approach to SSR.

While the government of Guinea Bissau decided to move forward in implementing the national security strategy, there were different hurdles to overcome. Amongst them was the need for accurate censuses for the military and the police forces. Together with the UN, the IfS team is contributing to the census process. It also supports the government in drawing up pension schemes and setting up funds for demobilisation and reintegration of military personnel. It also helps them to develop criteria for who will qualify for this kind of support.

The Commission expert team is advising the minister of defence who is responsible for the overall reform process and providing support to the technical committee that has been set up to implement the national security sector strategy. The team works closely with the Commission delegation to link the IfS activities with the long term plans under the EDF. The Commission's head of delegation is also playing a crucial role in the reform process and sits on the National Steering Committee for the SSR process.

The IfS team also helps in preparing the ground for the incoming EU mission under the European Security and Defence Policy (ESDP). The ESDP mission will give more specific advice in the areas of defence and police reform, as well as in the area of criminal justice.

Interaction with other actors on the ground is important. The fact that the range of donors is increasing is positive but also challenging. The growing international interest in the country means that the different actors raise expectations and give advice, but they do not necessarily mobilise sufficient financial resources which are needed for the long-term reform process.

In Guinea Bissau there is broad national consensus among the political leaders and in the armed forces of the need to go ahead with the SSR process. The momentum for reform is there. Given the drugs and corruption issues, however, it could change if the reform process is not progressing in the coming year.

With sea access and cashew nut production, Guinea Bissau is not suffering from a real humanitarian crisis and real hunger compared with other African countries. But the lack of infrastructure and electricity and the corruption issues make economic development very difficult.

Countries in post-conflict situations are quite often fragile politically and economically, so things are not moving quickly in Guinea Bissau. The Stability Instrument team has good field experience from other parts of Africa. They are aware that the reform process in the country will be a gradual one, and they will encourage the local authorities to move ahead with their efforts.

An undercover officer working on drug-related cases for the judicial police. The police say they are trying to do what they can to stop the influx of drugs but claims the government has left them with few resources.
© Rebecca Blackwell / AP Photo / Guinea Bissau

The most disturbing impediment to fighting serious crime is that Guinea Bissau has no prisons since the country's only one was destroyed in the civil war. This means that convicts and suspects have to be held together in cramped police cells. Consequently sentences are rarely longer than a few months even for the most serious crimes.

© Justin Sutcliffe / The Sunday Telegraph 2007 / Guinea Bissau

INTERVIEW | **JOAQUIM GOMES**
Instrument for Stability Advisor
to the Technical Committee

The EU's role in Guinea Bissau

Guinea Bissau is one of the signatory countries of the Cotonou Agreement, a treaty between the European Union and the group of African, Caribbean and Pacific (ACP) states, which aims at the reduction and eventual eradication of poverty while contributing to sustainable development and to the gradual integration of ACP countries into the world economy. In this context, the European Union is the most important donor to Guinea Bissau in financial terms with an annual disbursement of about €20–30 million in EDF funds alone.

Apart from its fight against poverty and for sustainable development in Guinea Bissau, the European Union also has some commercial interests in the country, especially in the fisheries sector, where a multi-annual agreement between the two parties exists.

New challenge, different problems

Despite my previous experience with EU security sector reform activities in Angola and in Iraq, this mission is a new challenge and the problems are different from the ones that I had to deal with in those places. The permanent lack of working material and working facilities and the very poor financial resources which are available to perform our tasks are the biggest difficulties that we are facing in Guinea Bissau.

However, this problem is to be solved soon once the rehabilitation of 'Institut National de Défense' (IND) is finished. Moreover, the signature of the convention with the EU (the SSR/DRR Project of €7.7 million) will provide the local authorities with the needed resources to move forward. And in order to prepare the census of the armed forces a sensitisation campaign has been planned and developed and has been applied to all military units within the country.

Step-by-step trust-building with the authorities

The relationships with the Guinea Bissau authorities are very friendly. Our presence and our job are well accepted and they follow most of our advice. Achieving this level of very good confidence, however, took quite some time and patience. We still have to make efforts to build an environment of mutual trust; it is a day-by-day process that moves step by step. Daily appointments and interviews on an ad-hoc basis and our permanent availability are being quietly appreciated.

Our main concern was to demonstrate the local authorities that we are here to help and work with them and not to work against them. The fact that I am Portuguese is a big plus in my job. This is especially due to the common language and cultural influence and to Guinea Bissau's traditional links to Portugal as its former colonial master.

'Qisa' (crack) addicts in a flophouse on the outskirts of Bissau. Qisa is the hidden cost of the rising drug traffic through Bissau. Local sellers are paid in cocaine and then have to sell it themselves to make a profit. Often it is cooked and turned into crack or qisa which doubles the yield and produces a powerful and addictive drug that is within the financial reach of the local population.

© Justin Sutcliffe / The Sunday Telegraph 2007 / Guinea Bissau

The military has enormous influence

While officially power is not with the armed forces, the influence of the military exceeds its legally defined competences in the country. That means that for coordination purposes all matters related to the military have to be addressed to the general chief of staff. And after discussing the issue and after getting his agreement, then things may move on.

The drugs phenomenon in Guinea Bissau is rather new. However, money made in the drugs trade is becoming more and more visible in the country, with luxury cars driving on the streets and new houses being built. The fact that Guinea Bissau is a transit point for drugs first became known three to four years ago.

But the speed of the country's transformation into a major entry point for South American cocaine has surprised the donor community. There are rumours and allegations in the press that high military and civil officials are involved in the drugs business. But concrete proof is hard to obtain in a situation where you have a very limited number of judicial police forces with limited resources to investigate.

INTERVIEW | KARL RAWERT
Head of Section, Economy, Trade and Regional Integration, EC Delegation to Guinea Bissau

Besides my tasks as Head of Section for Economy, Trade and Regional Integration in Guinea Bissau, I also deal with the European Commission's programmes in the fields of institutional support and SSR in the country.

Although the action under the IfS in Guinea Bissau is directly managed by our colleagues from DG RELEX in Brussels, the IfS experts give valuable assistance to our cooperation as a whole, in particular by preparing the ground for a large-scale EDF project with a budget of €7.7 million for SSR in Guinea Bissau.

One of the main objectives of the SSR is to create security forces that are supportive of the democratic systems instead of destabilising the country, as has been frequently the case in the past.

Working relations with the national authorities are generally good. The European Commission is widely recognized as a – if not *the* – major development partner for Guinea Bissau.

Lack of water and electricity, broken phone lines
Our team of three experts started their work in October 2007. For the first few months it has been all about establishing contacts and setting up an office, which in a country like Guinea Bissau is not that easy. We are facing

As an emergency measure the former finance ministry building has been converted to a makeshift detention centre. The dark basement houses the most dangerous convicts but nobody serves a sentence longer than four months due to overcrowding.
© Justin Sutcliffe / The Sunday Telegraph 2007 / Guinea Bissau

In the prisons there is virtually no daylight. Prisoners have no opportunity for exercise.
Mosquitoes feast in the perpetual twilight and few men have nets to sleep under.
Only the shortness of sentences has prevented an epidemic of tuberculosis.
© Justin Sutcliffe / The Sunday Telegraph 2007 / Guinea Bissau

difficulties in our daily work mainly because of logistical problems such as water and electricity which are also lacking in public administration facilities. International phone lines are not working properly, and often we cannot access the internet for a couple of days.

My daily work is also hampered by frequent delays in the payment of salaries for the civil servants. The public administration is oversized and only partially qualified for the tasks that it should perform and for the responsibilities that it should assume. However, this problem is not being tackled under the IfS, but with other EC and bilateral donor programmes.

Under the EC IfS, our team provides help to kick-start demobilisation and reintegration activities. A recently signed agreement of Commission support for SSR in Guinea Bissau is mainly focused on the support for demobilisation and for the economic and social integration of ex-military staff.

Overstaffed military forces

According to estimates and in terms of relative size to population, the number of military forces in Guinea Bissau, with 5.04 soldiers per 1,000 inhabitants, is significantly higher than in other countries in the region. In the member states of the West African Economic and Monetary Union (WAEMU), the average stands at 1.23 soldiers per 1,000 inhabitants.

Precise figures on the demobilisation of the military, however, will only be available after the completion of the armed forces census. One of the goals of SSR in Guinea Bissau is to downsize the defence sector from current numbers to a staff of 3,400 soldiers as set out in the national SSR strategy.

Find new jobs for demobilised people

The biggest challenges for us are to find new jobs for the demobilised people, to win the acceptance of the military chiefs and to secure sufficient funds for the overall implementation of the programme. The European Commission has no anti-drugs experts on the ground, but at a conference in Lisbon in December 2007 it pledged to earmark €2 million as a contribution to the national anti-drugs strategy.

It is evident that combating drug trafficking and also the fight against illegal immigration – two major problems in Guinea Bissau – can only be won in close cooperation with the national authorities. Other programmes aim at strengthening the judicial system and the rule of law. Hence, they will contribute directly and indirectly to the fight against drugs trafficking.

The fight against drug trafficking is being led by the Judiciary Police. They have just some 70 employees, who must also deal with all the country's domestic crime as well.
© Justin Sutcliffe / The Sunday Telegraph 2007 / Guinea Bissau

LEBANON

Support for the return and reintegration
of Palestinian refugees from Nahr el Bared camp

REPORTAGE BY JULIANE VON REPPERT-BISMARCK

PHOTOGRAPHS & CAPTIONS BY RAMZI HAIDA

Nahr el Bared, 22 May 2007
Palestinian family, in the back of a car fleeing the refugee camp in northern Lebanon.
After three days of ferocious fighting between Islamists and the Lebanese army, a truce sparked
a mass exodus from the Palestinian refugee camp which was the principal battleground.
© Ramzi Haidar / AFP PHOTO / Lebanon, Nahr el Bared

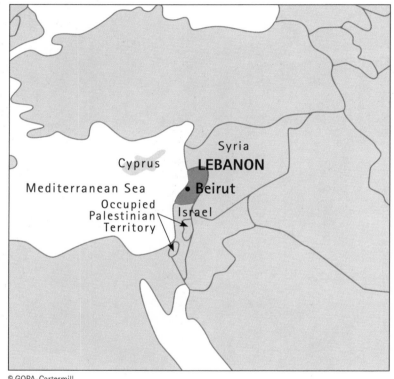

© GOPA-Cartermill

Capital: Beirut

Area: 10,400 km²

Population: 4,099,000 (2007)

Note: Includes about 395,000 non-naturalized Palestinian refugees, of which about 225,000 live in refugee camps.

Life expectancy at birth: male 70.2 years; female 75.2 years (2005)

Government type: unitary multiparty republic with one legislative house

GNI – per capita: US$ 5,342 (2006)

Source: © 2008 Encyclopædia Britannica, Inc.

INTRODUCTION

When Palestinian families first arrived in the rocky landscape of northern Lebanon in 1948, they prepared for a two-week stay on the edge of the sea. They had no idea they would be spending the next 60 years there, building a refugee camp whose alleyways would grow narrower as the population swelled to more than four times the density of Manhattan or Hong Kong. Nor did they know the end of their camp would come in the shape of a bloody four-month battle between Lebanese troops and Islamic radicals, obliterating the camp and leaving them homeless once again.

At 03.00 on Sunday 20 May 2007, Lebanese security forces launched surprise strikes into Nahr el Bared camp as a response to the jihadist militants known as Fatah al-Islam's attack on Lebanese soldiers. Within days the camp's 30,000 refugees fled the bombings, taking with them their barest belongings. Lebanon's target was Fatah al-Islam, an offspring of Syrian-backed Fatah al-Intifada widely believed to be inspired by al-Qaeda. Under the leadership of Palestinian-born Shaker al-Abssi, who had recently been released from prison in Syria and arrived in Lebanon, the group had entrenched itself in the camp thanks to a power vacuum created when Lebanon handed the policing of camps to Palestinians in 1969. Fatah al-Islam recruited new members from Syria, Afghanistan, Iraq and from within the scattered Palestinian community. Many had experience from the battlefields of Iraq, and they trained inside the camp under the averted eyes of a refugee population used to the ebb and flow of militias in their camp. However fierce the Lebanese onslaught, Fatah al-Islam held out for months, entrenching themselves in the narrow alleyways

Nahr el Bared, 22 May 2007
Palestinian refugees crossing to safety from the southern entrance of the besieged camp. The refugees fled the battered camp by foot, in cars or pickup trucks when the guns fell silent after three days of ferocious fighting between Islamist militiamen and the Lebanese army. The aim of the army shelling was to wipe out fighters from the al-Qaeda-inspired Sunni extremist group, Fatah al-Islam.
© Ramzi Haidar / AFP PHOTO / Lebanon, Nahr el Bared

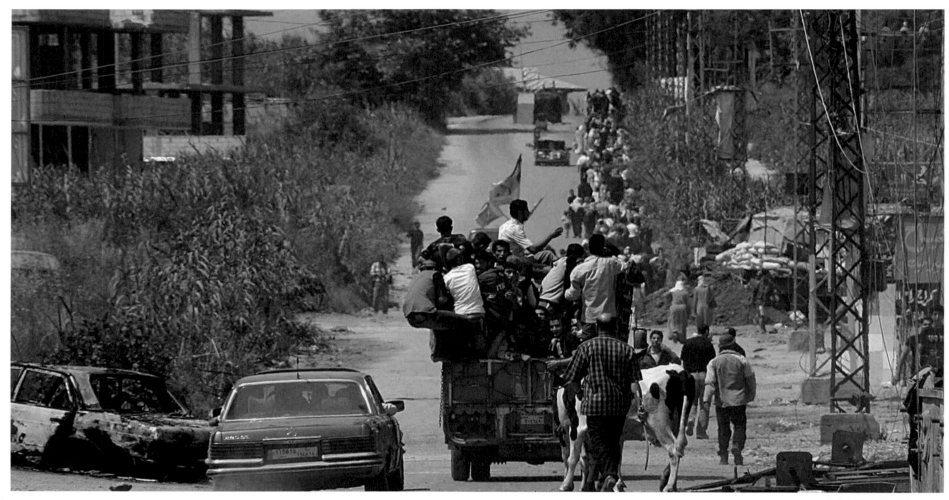

Nahr el Bared, 23 May 2007
Palestinian refugees are crossing to safety from the southern entrance of their besieged camp. The refugees fled the camp by foot, in cars or pickup trucks when the guns fell silent after three days of ferocious fighting between Islamist militiamen and the Lebanese army. The aim of the army shelling was to wipe out fighters from the al Qaeda-inspired Sunni extremist group, Fatah al-Islam.
© Ramzi Haidar / AFP PHOTO / Lebanon, Nahr el Bared

and interconnected buildings of the warren-like camp. By the time Lebanese troops defeated the last fighters 105 days later, 160 soldiers, 38 civilians and 200 militants were dead, according to the Lebanese government. The camp had been reduced to rubble piled 5 m high.

At the time of writing, the refugees have been living in emergency shelter for seven months. Having been moved out of their initial housing in garages and school yards of neighbouring Beddawi camp and Tripoli, they live in temporary housing and barracks in the area. They have swelled the already overcrowded Beddawi camp to twice its size. An uneasy truce exists between families of both camps. In areas on Lebanese territory now sheltering Palestinian refugees the tension is palpable. Palestinian families living in Lebanese schools were booed and hissed at the beginning of the school year; and as Lebanese families mourn the soldiers they lost in fighting in Nahr el Bared, Palestinian resentment simmers against a country that affords them few rights.

Lebanon has become the international litmus test for tensions in the Middle East. Former UN Secretary-General Kofi Annan last autumn described the situation in the Middle East as being at its most critical and dangerous stage ever. Within Lebanon tensions are palpable. Deadly car bomb attacks against leading politicians fuel political instability; tensions are on the rise between Lebanese and Palestinians in the north, and concerns are growing about militancy across Lebanon's refugee camps, notably Ain el Hilweh. Coming less than a year after the highly destructive Lebanese–Israeli summer war in 2006, the destruction of Nahr el Bared camp has thrown into sharp relief the need for state-imposed security in the camps; for measures to seal Lebanon's borders from destabilising outside forces; for improved living conditions and jobs for refugees, and for the mitigation of rising tensions between Palestinians and a Lebanese population caught up in a political crisis of their own.

Nahr el Bared, 26 May 2007
Palestinian refugees approaching a Lebanese army checkpoint fleeing the besieged camp. The Lebanese government offered the thousands of civilians trapped inside a chance to leave the camp after a couple of days of siege. Sniper fire had stopped all but a few dozens from fleeing as the Lebanese army put the militant group Fatah al-Islam under siege.
© Ramzi Haidar / AFP PHOTO / Lebanon, Nahr el Bared

RESOLVING THE CRISIS OF NAHR EL BARED CAMP

How to rebuild the camp has become one of the most pressing questions facing Lebanon and the international community amid rising security fears as Islamic radicals recruit among displaced and disillusioned Palestinians.

IfS currently supports three projects in Lebanon, each in collaboration with other international organisations and donor governments. One, worth €2 million, supports international efforts to secure Lebanon's northern border, a crucial step in reassuring Israel that Lebanon's borders are impermeable to disruptive outside influences. Another, worth €400,000, provides technical assistance to Lebanon's internal security forces. But the largest batch of money, €6.8 million, aims to help resolve the crisis of Nahr el Bared camp. Proposed in October 2007 and approved in December 2007, the project will be implemented by the United Nations Relief and Works Agency for Palestine Refugees in the Near East (UNRWA, pronounced UN-re-WA). UNRWA has been responsible since 1949 for direct relief and work programmes in refugee camps — running schools, building hospitals and clinics and checking sanitation, infrastructure and food supplies in the camps. UNRWA recently launched a drive to

Nahr el Bared, 26 May 2007
An elderly Palestinian woman is supported as she crosses a Lebanese army checkpoint while fleeing the besieged camp.
© Ramzi Haidar / AFP PHOTO / Lebanon, Nahr el-Bared

PROJECT FACTS & FIGURES

Programme
Support to the return and reintegration of Palestinian refugees from Nahr el Bared camp in Northern Lebanon

Location
Eastern Lebanon — Nahr el Bared old camp. This spans approximately 400,000 m² of land designated as camp territory, plus some adjacent land bought and leased informally from Lebanese landowners by the refugees.

Total IfS funds for Lebanon
(including border patrol projects)
€9.2 million

IfS funds for Nahr el Bared
€6.8 million, of which about €6 million is for searching, sorting and clearing rubble.

Project start on 15 March 2008

Project duration up until 26 June 2009

Partners
The project will collaborate with the United Nations Relief and Works Agency for Palestine Refugees in the Near East.

Volume of rubble to be cleared
500,000 m³ (according to UNRWA) – equivalent of filling Sydney Opera House about 19 times

Population density in old camp
1,100 inhabitants per ha, according to UNRWA. This is equivalent to 110,000 residents per km²: four times the density of Manhattan (25,000 in 2000), and denser than Gaza (about 74,000).

PROJECT OBJECTIVES

To prepare and facilitate the return and progressive reintegration of 30,000 Palestinian refugees displaced by the battle for Nahr el Bared camp in Northern Lebanon.

Specific objectives:

- to assess the situation, expectation and needs of displaced refugees from Nahr el Bared currently living in temporary accommodation in and around Beddawi camp and near the battle site.
- to fund the removal of 500,000 m³ of rubble.
- to form a planning committee and fund the creation of a masterplan that will be used for the reconstruction of the camp.
- to support business projects and microfinance initiatives among the refugees.

improve infrastructure and public services in Palestinian refugee camps across the Middle East, and before the siege had started drawing up a detailed picture of life and housing in Nahr el Bared. Little did UNRWA know how important this information gathering would be some months later. Channelled through UNRWA, the European Union's €6.8 million package aims to do four things:

- It aims to assess the situation, expectation and needs of displaced refugees from Nahr el Bared currently living in temporary accommodation in and around Beddawi camp and near the battle site.

- It will pay for the removal of 500,000 m³ of rubble. This volume of cement and detritus is all that remains of the camp. The rubble removal will happen only after refugees have searched for remains of private possessions and the rubble has been sorted according to toxicity. The rubble clearing is slated to take between three and six months; it is not clear how long it will take to search and sort it beforehand.

- It has helped form a planning committee and is funding the creation by the committee of a masterplan that will be used for the reconstruction of the camp. The planning group includes architects and EU and UN experts funded by the European Union, as well as a grassroots committee of Nahr el Bared refugees and representatives of the Lebanese government and army. This mix is seen as crucial for ensuring a harmonious recovery of the region.

- It will support with business projects and microfinance initiatives among others the refugees' efforts to rebuild their shops and businesses on the road to economic recovery. This is particularly important given urgent measures to seal the nearby Lebanese–Syrian border. Palestinians and Lebanese in the region have until now plied a booming trade in oil, vegetables, grain and industrial goods smuggled across the Syrian border.

Nahr el Bared, 26 May 2007
A Palestinian man drives his bullet-struck car out of the besieged camp.
© Ramzi Haidar / AFP PHOTO / Lebanon, Nahr el Bared

INTERVIEW | **RICHARD COOK**
Director of UNRWA Affairs in Lebanon
for Palestine Refugees in the Middle East

Current situation for Palestinians in Nahr el Bared camp

I've spent a total of ten years in the Occupied Territories and many more in the Middle East. I oversaw Gaza's construction programmes in the 1990s which aimed to bring to Palestinian people the results of peace following the 1993 Oslo Accords. Since then I've overseen the building of infrastructure, schools, clinics and hospitals in many camps.

But in all my time working with Palestinians, I have found that refugees' living conditions here in Lebanon are consistently at the level of the worst I've seen anywhere. Palestinian refugees here have been excluded from normal civil rights. They are not allowed to participate in dozens of occupations. They cannot be engineers, doctors, pharmacists or lawyers. Since they do not have their own state, the Palestinians cannot offer Lebanon any reciprocal agreement on employment to make their situation better. In 2001 they lost the right to own property outside the camps, or to pass property that they owned before 2001 to their children. They can get around this by registering their property in the name of a Lebanese citizen, but even that is a risk. Syria and Jordan provide secondary education for Palestinians, but that is not the case in Lebanon. Unemployment amongst Palestinian refugees is high. If they do find legal work in construction or in agriculture, Palestinians in Lebanon have no right to a pension, health insurance or social services, and there is no provision of health, education or relief for them outside what they get from UNRWA.

The first thing that strikes you about the camps is that they are incredibly overcrowded, which is a result of the area of the camp not expanding over the years even though the population has increased fourfold.

The result is a high level of poverty and an inability for Palestinians to change their own environment. You will come across an old couple living in a shelter without sanitation, electricity or water, sleeping on the earth floor under a roof made of corrugated iron. There is no ventilation, a lack of natural light and the place is infested with vermin. This is not an isolated incident: you will find this sort of thing in any refugee camp in Lebanon. UNRWA has estimated in the past that 11.8 per cent of Palestinian refugees in Lebanon live in abject poverty — compared with 8.6 per cent in Gaza. It's inevitable that the conditions you see in the camps lead to unemployment, and like in any inner city in Britain or in Europe, they are vulnerable to crime, or in this case to extremism. In many cases it's the only way they can get an income for their families.

Resolving the situation of displaced refugees from the camp

The refugees from Nahr el Bared have this incredible will, this incredible need to go back. One woman told me, 'I accept that I will not go back to my home in Israel, but I do not accept that I won't go back to my camp.' The people are frustrated and scared of what will happen. They're worried that they will be permanently displaced. The tension is evident whenever I meet with the refugees, and have to ask them to be patient while we sort through the rubble of their camp to make sure that there are no more unexploded devices.

Nahr el Bared, 23 June 2007
Smoke from artillery and tank shelling rises from the Palestinian Nahr el Bared refugee camp.
Lebanese troops bombarded the Islamist militants ending a sustained siege lasting nearly five weeks.
© Ramzi Haidar / AFP PHOTO / Lebanon, Nahr el Bared

During the summer months many of the 30,000 refugees were mainly living in schools and public places in neighbouring Beddawi camp and Tripoli, but that had to change, particularly once school started in the autumn. The tension between residents and the refugees was growing. Now we're giving 3,000 families rental subsidies for a maximum of three to five months, but that outlay can't be sustained. We're also bringing in temporary prefabricated housing units – much of that using funding from the European Union's humanitarian aid programme – and refurbishing buildings on land near the camp to provide additional accommodation. Some of the families have gone to the areas adjacent to the camp – into conditions with no water or electricity, where sewers and roads are damaged. Now in winter there is a lot of rain, and it's getting very muddy there. We recognise that these are not the conditions for people to go back to, but we have had to facilitate it right now, for symbolic reasons.

There is also the issue of rising tension between the refugees and the Lebanese. The current Lebanese government under Lebanese Prime Minister Fouad Siniora has done much to improve the conditions for the Palestinians. But in the streets there are still many who blame the Palestinians for the country's civil war. As far as they are concerned, improving the living conditions of Palestinians is a bad thing because it increases the likelihood that they will want to stay.

Logistical and legal challenges ahead
We urgently need to find out what to do about the rubble. We've cleared one-tenth of it, but there are another 450,000 m³ to go. The Lebanese army has a site, but we can only use this if it is sound from an environmental point of view.

Beddawi refugee camp, 20 July 2007
Palestinian refugees from the Nahr el Bared camp rest at a nearby camp. They have been stripped of virtually all their belongings; their houses, their livelihood, their precious jewellery and even their identity papers.
© Ramzi Haidar / AFP PHOTO / Lebanon, Nahr el Bared

We have to divide the rubble into toxic and non-toxic waste and make sure we dispose of it safely. The EU funds are paying for the UN Development Programme to bring in environmental experts to check on this.

Then there is the issue of land rights. The camp's 30,000 residents were mainly living on an area that spans 400,000 m² – approximately the size of 48 large football fields. That land still belongs to the Lebanese families who leased it to the Lebanese government in 1948, and those families are now demanding either to have their land back or to be paid a market price for it. This would cost the Lebanese government about US$ 6 million which it doesn't currently have. We hope this will be resolved soon, so that we can start clearing rubble and prepare to rebuild the camp.

There are UNRWA staff, experts from the American University of Beirut and Palestinian architects working with EU funds to co-design the camp masterplan. A lot of our time is spent negotiating the design with the refugees, the Lebanese government and the army. Lebanese Prime Minister Siniora wants to address security concerns and he wants a quick rebuilding process to limit the potential of tensions flaring up. But he won't give the refugees more land than they got when they arrived here in 1948, even though the population has multiplied fourfold since then. So we are looking for a formula that will allow us to put the same amount of people onto the same area of land as before while at the same time improving their living conditions and creating open spaces and making streets wide enough for police patrols and ambulances. It's virtually an impossible task. We're talking about one of the most densely populated urban areas in the world, denser than Bombay, Shanghai or Hong Kong. The answer is of course to build a higher-rise camp, with houses that have more floors than before. But there we have another problem: the army is concerned about tall buildings and staircases being hard to control in case there is fighting in the future. It is a very difficult discussion we are having.

A blueprint for future similar situations

The army has had a bad experience with Nahr el Bared. I don't think for a moment that they would want to go through that again here in Lebanon. But sadly we're likely to have a chance in the future in other parts of the Middle East to use the lessons we've learned here. And even in a peaceful situation we will be able to use these lessons for camp improvements, like in Neirab camp near Aleppo in Syria: we know more now about how to address environmental issues, overcrowding and collapsing infrastructure. We know about bomb disposal and mass rubble clearing. And in future emergencies we will be better prepared to find experts and donors and create supply chains.

We are already using this project as an opportunity to improve women's rights, by including them in the discussions of how to improve the camp. We should also use this as an example of what can be done to get young unemployed people into jobs. We will be able to use part of the EU funds to launch microfinance programmes that will stimulate economic recovery and bring opportunity to the camp's youth.

The crucial issue is that Nahr el Bared should not be treated in isolation but that its reconstruction be taken as part of the broader improvement of the lives of Palestinians. Yes, the families of Nahr el Bared have suffered extraordinarily. But there is frustration and anger everywhere. And that makes young people vulnerable to extremism.

Nahr el Bared, 12 August 2007
Black smoke rises amid severely damaged buildings at the Nahr al Bared camp.
Lebanese soldiers are being hampered in their fight against holed-up Islamist
militants by the stench of putrefying corpses making the air unbreathable.

© Ramzi Haidar / AFP PHOTO / Lebanon, Nahr el Bared

Nahr el Bared, 20 September 2007
A Lebanese soldier walks towards the destroyed Nahr el Bared refugee camp
after the bombings. The Fatah al-Islam militant group may have been crushed by
the army after 15 weeks of fierce battles but people from nearby villages remain
fearful as the militia's leader is still on the run.
© Ramzi Haidar / AFP PHOTO / Lebanon, Nahr el Bared

INTERVIEW | **MUNA BUDEIRI Head of the Housing and Camp Improvement Unit, UNRWA Infrastructure and Camp Improvement Department**

Building on prior experiences in the reconstruction of Nahr el Bared

When my bosses at UNRWA called me and said, 'You shall help rebuild Nahr el Bared,' the first thing I thought was that these people have lost 60 years of their efforts. They have lost the house they built for their daughter, their shop, the new floor they'd constructed for their son, their diplomas, every trace of their lives.

The thing that struck me about Nahr el Bared camp when I visited it before the bombings was that its residents were always doing more, always working at making their lives better. No house in Nahr el Bared ever ended with a roof. The ceiling always ended with columns reaching up into the sky so residents could add another floor once they'd saved up enough money for the building materials. That possibility of improving their lot, of expanding their living space upwards when they were not allowed to expand sideways onto new land, that is very important to the refugees.

I hadn't been prepared for what I saw when I went into the camp with a UN convoy after the fighting ended. It is not just shocking. It's unbelievable. Everything is on the ground. It's like a world war has happened and at the same time an earthquake. There is not a square metre that hasn't been flattened. You see bits of furniture, children's books, half-burned clothing on clothes lines hanging on the fallen-down columns of buildings. An old lady said to me, 'I don't know what we've done in our lives to deserve all this torture, being refugees over and over again.'

Nahr el Bared, 28 September 2007
Lebanese soldiers patrol in an armoured vehicle around the devastated Palestinian refugee camp after the bombings have ceased. The fighting against Fatah al-Islam al-Qaeda inspired militants in and around the camp, which lasted from 20 May 2007 to 2 September 2007, and cost about 400 lives. All of Nahr el Bared's 31,000 residents fled the camp to seek refuge in some of the country's other 11 refugee camps.
© Ramzi Haidar / AFP PHOTO / Lebanon, Nahr el Bared

Seeking advice from the refugees

From our side there are architects, designers, planners, urban design experts, researchers and technical experts involved in designing the camp. The refugees were suspicious when we started asking them for input on the camp design. They feared we would tell them what to do. I told them, 'I need you to work with me. I need at the end of the day to have your buy-in.' It is crucial to have the input of the community. We cannot sit in our offices and decide what's best for them. We need to talk to them and listen to them, we need to do surveys to understand how these people's lives worked.

For anyone visiting the camp, it may look as if camps like Nahr el Bared are not organised; that they are chaotic and unstructured. The alleyways are often so narrow that you can't even open an umbrella. When people died in Nahr el Bared it was often impossible to carry them out in a stretcher because there simply was no space. When you walked through the streets and looked up you would see balconies bumping into each other, overlapping from opposing buildings, forming bridges. Many rooms in family buildings didn't have any windows, and during the winter rains the damp of the camp was terrible.

But the reality is that the residents have organised things for 60 years: how to deal with external public space, with disputes over property and things like balconies. They've learned to manage problems that arise from not being able to legally expand their town outside the limits laid 60 years ago. They've put in place mechanisms to survive with limited economic means. And they've reconstructed to an extent the feel and personal networks of the villages they left in 1948. The different parts of the camp carry the names of their former home villages and towns: Safad, Damoun, Safouri, Sasa, Jahoula.

Nahr el Bared, 10 October 2007
Lebanese soldiers search a Palestinian refugee before he enters camp. Dozens of Palestinian families returned in buses and mini-vans hired by the UN Relief and Works Agency with just a few personal items.
© Ramzi Haidar / AFP PHOTO / Lebanon, Nahr el Bared

So to understand how all this works I went looking for a link to the community when I started on the project. Luckily there was already something like that: a grassroots committee called the Nahr el Bared Reconstruction Commission, whose members are the residents of the camp; engineers, professionals and also modest people and women all having their say.

With them we organised meetings with residents of the camp to gather an exact picture of what the camp was like before the bombing: the size of the buildings, streets, the location of shops. We divided the camp into sections and called in people section by section. We made them sit together and with social workers and engineers got them to reconstruct the camp through telling what was in each house, how big were the rooms, how many kitchens, how many bathrooms. We had them talk until they had agreed every last detail of how the camp was divided up.

We were lucky with Nahr el Bared — before the bombings UNRWA had started preparing for an improvement programme in the camp. So we already had some data about the camp, the layout, streets and population density.

Reconstructing elements of the past

What is important for them is the extended family approach. Families in Nahr el Bared lived together in single buildings. This allowed them to cope with economic hardship in a way that would be impossible in a rented flat among strangers. If there wasn't enough fuel for heating, a family would heat just one room and share that room. And they liked to have a rooftop of their own because it was a place for them to sit together at night in a city where there are almost no public spaces. It also gave them security in terms of an ability to house a growing population within the limits of the camp: when a new generation arrived in the family, they would build another floor.

We need to respect this in the master plan for the reconstruction for the camp. We need to keep existing neighbourhood structures together. We need to reconstruct, as far as possible, the living quarters and shopping streets as they were before. The refugees want to feel that when they go back to the camp the landmarks they remember are still there — the big shopping street that cut through the camp for instance, where people could do their shopping on their way home; the gold market; the shops that sold building materials, tiles, ceramics and food.

We're trying to do all of this: improve the community's living conditions and security standards, create public spaces and wider roads and at the same time keep to the confines of the original camp as the proposal to increase the camp area was rejected. Our solution right now is to make the camp taller than before. The average floor number will have not two or three floors as before, but three or four floors.

Avoiding the pitfalls of rebuilding efforts

We're under great pressure to deliver a master plan as soon as possible. This has to do with the bad current living conditions of the camp's displaced refugees, and with a need to prevent tensions between them and the residents in the areas where they now live. But the negotiation for the master plan is a very rough job because all the stakeholders — the refugees, the government, UNRWA, the army, the experts — have their own concerns and constraints. The army for instance is worried about the road network with easy accessibility in case of security or emergencies.

Of course the refugee community realises that things will have to change: they have agreed that those with bigger houses may have to give up 15 per cent or even more of their living space to make space for wider streets and proper ventilation. They know that with our design their houses will seem more spacious even if they are smaller. Some people who are living in very bad conditions – families of ten living in 50 m² of space – will get more space in the rebuilt camp. The community has agreed to this.

But we have to make sure we do not choose an approach which can have bad consequences in the long term. There are some cases to bear in mind. In

Gaza, for instance, there have been projects to build 10 and 11-floor buildings where people live alongside strangers. It's led to all sorts of social problems within the community. We have to avoid that: we have to listen to them so that the solution we find in the end is one they have agreed, and with which they can live.

Nahr el Bared, 10 October 2007
Palestinian refugee children show their identity cards as they wait for Lebanese soldiers to search their belongings before they enter the bombed-out Nahr el Bared refugee camp. Dozens of Palestinian families returned in buses and mini-vans hired by the UN Relief and Works Agency with just a few personal items.
© Ramzi Haidar / AFP PHOTO / Lebanon, Nahr el Bared

INTERVIEW | **PATRICK LAURENT**
            | **Head of EC Delegation to Lebanon**

Addressing security concerns and emergencies in Nahr el Bared

It came as no surprise to us when Lebanon started launching attacks on the camp in May. When I arrived to take my post in Beirut in November 2006, we spotted the threat very quickly: there was evidence of a massive inflow of terrorists into Nahr el Bared. We could not specify where they were coming from, but we could see the threat coming in.

Fatah al-Islam tried to enter Beddawi first but got chased away by local militias. So they tried Nahr el Bared and succeeded. They were a small group then, 20 people in total perhaps. They came with an awful lot of money, which allowed them to insert themselves nicely into the camp. They could offer marriage to local Palestinian girls and give the families endowments of between US$ 5,000 and US$ 10,000. That's a huge amount of money for people there, so gradually they were accepted. The source of the money is not clear. It is clear that once Fatah al-Islam's first members established themselves in the camp they started to recruit over the internet – young men from Syria, Saudi Arabia, Palestine and from Iraq. Some of them had a lot of experience fighting in Iraq.

In general, the camps in Lebanon are a fertile place for hiding. They have had no Lebanese law since the 1969 Cairo Agreement between the Palestinian Liberation Organisation and Lebanon, in which Lebanon handed over law enforcement to the Palestinians themselves in the camps. Needless to say that the living conditions in the camps compound the Palestinians' frustrations.

In Nahr el Bared, the Palestinians gradually realised that these people were starting to play them against each other, undermining the power of Hamas and Fatah who until now had been governing the camp. The vast majority of the resident refugees are not militant, and they realised they'd allowed a factor of insecurity into the camp. But by the time they realised, the devil was in the apple.

An unbalanced society

When I first visited Lebanon in 1972 it was a kind of small paradise, a Switzerland of the Middle East, financially and politically. This was a place where there was a happy coexistence between Christians, Shiites and Sunnis and many other faiths. What I found when I came back in 2006 was that it is a country that has such a weak state structure that it can easily be unbalanced. It recovered after the end of the civil war in 1990, but the 30 Days War with Israel in 2006 has undone a lot of that. There has been paralysis in government since November 2006 until May 2008, when President Michel Sleiman was elected. There are very few state elements that could take on the task of confronting a terrorism threat in a refugee camp – particularly since the camps have been allowed to govern themselves since 1969.

The last strong part of the state apparatus is the army. So it is not surprising that they were the ones in the end to take on Fatah al-Islam.

From grief to rebuilding

Come to see the camp and you will be shocked. I've never seen anyone who has seen it and who hasn't been silent for a long time afterwards. There is nothing left. There is a lot of dust and a few pillars. It's a very emotive sight. It's very serious, in terms of human needs and in political terms. We are talking of the complete destruction of a place where 30,000 people lived – that's a mid-sized town in Germany, or a big suburb of Paris.

So once the army is sure that there are no undetonated shells or mortar

Nahr el Bared, 11 October 2007
A Palestinian refugee carries his new born child
past Lebanee soldiers returning home to the bombed-out refugee camp.
© Ramzi Haidar / AFP PHOTO / Lebanon, Nahr el-Bared

bombs under the rubble we are going to give the refugees the chance to search for their belongings. They still have hope that they will find a picture of their aunt or parent, some personal souvenir of their family. It may be dangerous and it will be time-consuming, but it is part of the process of grieving for their loss. It is humanly necessary to let them search. They may not find anything but at least they have to be given the chance to try to find it.

Once we do start removing the rubble to a site that's been approved by the government and by environmental experts, it will take a long time to clear. There will be a continuous line of trucks carting the rubble out, and it will take at least several months to accomplish.

Involvement of European experts at all levels

The €6.8 million is going to be spent not only on the rubble removal. It will also pay for specialist architects, town mapping, engineers specialising in water and infrastructure. In the coming weeks we are going to finance the placement of long-term expertise close to the prime minister, to help developing a reconstruction Master Plan. It is very important to have an emergency fund such as the IfS. It is the only funding source that is providing for extremely fast mobilisation of funds. Traditional EU aid, and this is true for any donor, is like an oil tanker. It's big and important, but it is not agile. An oil tanker takes 20 nautical miles to change direction. It's the same for financial tools. The IfS is fast and adaptable. We asked for the money in October and had it in December. With that, the European Union is the only donor to be able to give this amount of money this quickly.

Nahr el Bared, 11 October 2007
A Palestinian refugee family check out what is left of their home. Dozens of Palestinian families
returned to Nahr el Bared from the Beddawi refugee camp where they had sought refuge.
© Ramzi Haidar / AFP PHOTO / Lebanon, Nahr el Bared

A broader vision for reconstruction and stabilisation in Lebanon

You see, the destruction of the camp has had an impact not only on the Palestinians. The camp used to be a place of consumption with regional ramification, and its destruction has destroyed many Lebanese livelihoods too. We need to make sure we alleviate the friction between the Lebanese and the Palestinians. The Lebanese were getting furious for example with refugees living in Lebanese school buildings. And even now that the schools are back to serving the Lebanese community, the inhabitants have a strange feeling vis-à-vis the Palestinians. They consider the Palestinians illegitimate settlers and yet they see that the international community is doing a lot for them. They are envious of the money that is going to be given to them. So we need to mitigate the risk of friction. We are going to allocate €18 million — that's not part of the IfS — to the development of northern Lebanon. Nahr el Bared has crystallised for us the awareness that something needs to be done in the impoverished north if the country is to be stable.

The funds going to Nahr el Bared now are just one of three projects funded by the IfS. The three all have at their core the goal of stabilising the area, and they reinforce each other. Beyond the €6.8 million for the camp, €2 million is going towards co-funding with international government donors the creation of a border patrol along the Lebanese border with Syria. This is a crucial element in assuring Lebanon's neighbours that it is capable of controlling its borders and the country itself. Beyond stopping the movement of dangerous people and weapons into Lebanon, the security project will also stop the flow of flour, petrol and other daily goods that are currently being smuggled into Lebanon. That will of course affect the livelihoods of those Lebanese and Palestinians who have made their living selling these goods. The economic recovery programme for Nahr el Bared, which will help refugees back into jobs, is crucial in addressing this side-effect of securing Lebanon's borders.

OCCUPIED PALESTINIAN TERRITORY

Support of Palestinian–Israeli negotiations towards a peace agreement

REPORTAGE BY MARIA-LAURA FRANCIOSI

PHOTOGRAPHS & CAPTIONS BY ALEXANDRA BOULAT

The Second Intifada. A dove lands near Israeli soldiers as the temporary lifting of a curfew comes to an end
in the West Bank town of Ramallah. Reacting to a wave of deadly suicide attacks, Israel launched its biggest
military offensive in over 20 years by reoccupying major cities in the West Bank and isolating Palestinian
leader Yasser Arafat in his Ramallah compound.
© Alexandra Boulat / Agence VII

Mediterranean Sea

Lebanon

OCCUPIED PALESTINIAN TERRITORY

Israel

Ramallah

Jordan

Egypt

© GOPA-Cartermill

Temporary Seat of Government: Ramallah
Area: 6,220 km2
Population: 4,008,332 (2007)
Life expectancy at birth: male 72 years; female 75 years
Government type: Parliamentary Democracy
GNI – per capita: US$ 1,120 (World Bank, 2006)

Source: © BBC

A Palestinian bound for Jerusalem crosses the Kalandia checkpoint near Ramallah in the West Bank, April 20, 2002. The checkpoint, one of the largest Israeli military checkpoints in the West Bank, separates Ramallah residents from southern Palestinian towns and the northern Palestinian neighborhoods of Jerusalem.
© Alexandra Boulat / Agence VII

INTRODUCTION

The EU has been working with the Palestinian Authority to build up the institutions of a future democratic, independent and viable Palestinian State living side by side with Israel and its neighbours. These efforts are regularly debated by the EU Council of Ministers.

The Action Plan concluded with the Palestinian Authority set up the agenda of the economic and political cooperation with the EU. The legal basis for the EU's relations with the PA is the Interim Association Agreement on Trade and Cooperation signed with the PLO on behalf of the Palestinian Authority.

The European Commission is the biggest donor of financial assistance to the Palestinians. The Commission suggested a series of ideas about a comprehensive strategy for assistance in its Communication to the Council and the European Parliament on 5 October 2005.

The EU believes that a two-state solution arrived at through negotiation is the best way to guarantee both Israel's security and the legitimate rights of the Palestinians. It is moreover in Europe's most vital interests to foster stability and prosperity in the whole Mediterranean region – including the Middle East – and the EU has committed considerable resources to this broad goal through the European Neighbourhood Policy (ENP). Under the ENP, Europe has become the leading external actor in the Palestinian state-building process and has deepened its political and economic ties to Israel.

Palestinian members of a Hamas militia pray at the Zeitun mosque after withdrawing from the streets of Gaza City, Friday, May 26, 2006.
© Alexandra Boulat / Agence VII

The EU also contributes to the peace process through its diplomatic efforts and in particular, through its participation in the Quartet (which also includes the United States, the United Nations and Russia), its bilateral relations with countries in the region and the Euro-Mediterranean Partnership, which remains the only multilateral forum outside the UN where all parties to the conflict can meet. The EU co-sponsored the Roadmap for Peace in June 2002 and contributes to all aspects of its implementation. The EU also sponsors initiatives bringing together civil society actors from Israel, the occupied Palestinian territory and neighbouring countries through the EU Partnership for Peace programme.

The EU is making a growing contribution to security in the OPT through EUPOL COPPS (the EU Police Coordinating Office for Palestinian Police Support). The mission has a long term reform focus and provides enhanced support to the Palestinian Authority in establishing sustainable and effective policing arrangements.

Since the establishment of the Palestinian Authority in 1994, the EU has provided more than €500m per year (Commission and Member States combined). From 1994 to 2000, assistance was primarily focused on development cooperation with a view to advancing the Palestinian state-building process. With the outbreak of the second intifada and the concomitant decline in social and economic conditions in the Occupied Palestinian Territory (OPT), EU assistance had to be largely re-oriented towards direct budget support to the PA and meeting the urgent humanitarian needs of the population. The EU now hopes to make development cooperation rather than humanitarian aid once again the primary focus of

European assistance to the OPT. By promoting good governance and human security, EU assistance contributes to social and political stability in the OPT, enhances the viability of the Palestinian state-in-waiting and bolsters the Palestinian Authority as a negotiating partner in the peace process. Assistance is also a key aspect of the EU's contribution to the implementation of the Roadmap whose first two phases call for Palestinian political reform, institution-building and economic recovery supported by the international community. The EU is also active in promoting initiatives that bring together representatives of Israeli and Palestinian civil society, as well as those from neighbouring countries, through its Partnership for Peace programme. EU financial assistance to the Palestinian Authority has also already led to vastly improved public finance management.

At the request of the Fayyad government, the Temporary International Mechanism (TIM) which the EU created in 2006 in order to provide aid directly to the Palestinian people, was extended until March 2008. TIM has now been replaced by a mechanism called PEGASE (French acronym: 'Mécanisme Palestino-Européen de Gestion de d'Aide Socio-Economique').The TIM has been a lifeline to ordinary Palestinians and their families both in the West Bank and in Gaza Strip. Since July 2007, the TIM has worked in close coordination with the PA government. The EC has moreover resumed direct technical assistance to the Palestinian Authority in the form of training and equipment.

The European Commission continues to provide humanitarian and food aid as well as emergency assistance to all Palestinians,

PROJECT FACTS & FIGURES

Programme
Support of Palestinian-Israeli negotiations towards a peace agreement

Location
Occupied Palestinian Territory

Total eligible cost of the action
€7,500,000

Project start
January 2008

Duration
18 months (from Jan. 2008)

Partner(s)
UN Development Programme (UNDP) and UN Office for Project Services (UNOPS)

including those in Gaza. Aid is provided to Palestinian refugees through UNRWA and to other organisations selected by DG ECHO. The EU also contributes to the World Bank project to repair the Beit Lahia sewage treatment centre. The untreated water accumulating in an artificial lake there had become a very serious health hazard for people living in that part of Gaza.

Aid is also provided directly to beneficiaries via the PEGASE mechanism, established in February 2008 by the European Commission to channel assistance to the building of the Palestinan state.

PEGASE channels support for the three year Palestinian Reform and Development Plan (PRDP) which was presented by the PA Prime Minister Salam Fayyad at the Paris Donor Conference of 17 December 2007. PEGASE supports a broad array of activities in the four priority sectors of the PRDP:
• Governance: fiscal reform, rule of law, justice, accountability, security;
• Social Development: social protection, health, education (including vocational education and training), employment schemes and the provision of basic supplies like fuel;

Happy Hamas supporters parade to celebrate the Hamas victory at Palestinian Legislative elections in Gaza, January 2006.
© Alexandra Boulat / Agence VII

Hamas supporters in a rally for the Palestinian Legislative election in Gaza, Jan. 2006.
© Alexandra Boulat / Agence VII / Palestine

PROJECT AIMS

To support the efforts of non-state actors, the United Nations and the Quartet, to promote confidence-building and reconciliation through the work of the Quartet Representative.

Specific objective:
- facilitating mediation in the peace process by providing operational and logistic support to the Office of the Quartet Representative and his staff based in Jerusalem

- improving operational performance of the Palestinian civil police

Expected results:
Promote an end to the conflict in conformity with the Road Map.

- Economic and Private Sector Development: trade facilitation, small and medium enterprises guarantee and financing, and business centres;
- Public Infrastructure Development in areas such as water, environment or energy.

PEGASE builds upon the work of the Temporary International Mechanism (TIM). However, while the TIM was an emergency assistance mechanism renewed every three-month, PEGASE is an instrument covering a wider range of activities and lasting three years, the same period as the PRDP.

PEGASE support to the PRDP is complemented by the EC programmes devoted to Palestinian refugees through UNRWA and Non State Actors including International NGOs as well as by the humanitarian and food aid programmes of ECHO.

Beit Hanun after the Israeli Autumn Clouds military operation which left 65 people dead in a week time, North of Gaza, November 14. 2006.

The West Bank and the Separation Wall. Sheep walk along a road next to the separation wall between Israel and the occupied Palestinian territory in Bethlehem, on March 19, 2007.
© Alexandra Boulat / Agence VII

Women sit to talk inside their destroyed house, in the rubble of Jenin refugee camp.
© Alexandra Boulat / Agence VII

Fearing more clashes, young Fatah gunmen of the El Jorf family take position on the roof of their home in Gaza, May 26, 2006. Mohamad El Jorf was killed on May 8, 2006 in clashes between Fatah activists and members of the Izzedeen El-Qassam Brigades (the armed wing of Hamas). Death squad leader Rassam El Jorf was also injured in Khan Yunis, Gaza.
© Alexandra Boulat / Agence VII

INTERVIEW | **NADIM KARKUTLI**
Crisis Response Planner
(Middle East and North Africa)
EC Directorate General for External Relations

The nature of the IfS

The Financial Decision for the IfS programme in support of Israeli–Palestinian negotiations was adopted shortly before Christmas 2007. It was largely and immediately in response to the positive outcome of the Annapolis meeting, held in November, between the Palestinian Authority (PA) and Israel, the Arab states, the United States and the international community, and the Paris Conference in December of the same year. In Paris the international donor community pledged to give US\$ 7 billion over several years in assistance to the Palestinians and to reinvigorate and reawaken the peace process.

Therefore our programme is the first rapid reaction, if you wish, in particular areas that cannot be covered by the 'normal' assistance programme of the European Union: 'normal' being continuing support.

Our EU mission in Ramallah identified that the police equipment was largely dilapidated or destroyed, and that there was individual capacity (although obviously further training was needed), but the most urgent need was for equipment. There are so many police stations that have no telephone, computer, patrol cars or integrated functioning communications, and so we shall give a sort of first kick-start contribution to finance equipment such as communications, cars and IT. Our delegation in Jerusalem will sign a contract with the UN Office for Project Services, which has been chosen by the PA and us as the implementing partner.

In a crisis situation like this it is permitted to negotiate directly with one or two suppliers and immediately buy the equipment needed instead of going for international competitive procurement. We hope to show a good example of how the IfS works well in practice. We quickly make the money available; we quickly sign the contract with the partner, and we can then rapidly do what we need without having to resort to normal procurement procedures. It must be pointed out though that this is only a fraction of the overall EU external aid budget, and these rules are enshrined by the Council, the Member States and the Parliament.

Now the other element is a direct contribution for the mission of the Quartet Representative, former UK Prime Minister Tony Blair. The Quartet partners have been called upon to share the burden. The United Nations is doing a lot of the logistics; one Quartet partner manages the operation on behalf of Mr. Blair and the Quartet. Technically we have become a policy office to his team, and have now decided to make available €2.5 million which will largely cover the running costs for 18 months, including the office costs in Jerusalem, which will bring our share of the overall operation to about one third of the total costs. The United States and Russia have also made pledges to support the team financially, and they have also seconded personnel. Additional funds have been contributed by Norway and bilaterally by the United Kingdom. So it is a multi-donor effort. We have to provide our share, which we do.

INTERVIEW | **ANDREA MATTEO FONTANA**
**International Relations Officer – Occupied–
Palestinian Territory (OPT), EC Directorate–
General for External Relations**

Financing the Palestinian police

The security issue is the key area of the conflict: if you want to tackle the security of Israel you also have to tackle the security in the West Bank and Gaza. And therefore we have to help the PA to be able to convince Israel that they can guarantee security on their own. This is not the case so far. We want the PA to go back to the years before the intifada when they were controlling all the urban centres, not only Nablus. The recent deployment of Palestinian policemen in Nablus is a good example. The PA deployed new retrained policemen, managed to collect weapons and reduce violence. But then what happened? Because Israel was not fully convinced that this is working, several incursions in Nablus undermined the efforts of the PA. Nevertheless, the security situation has considerably improved.

So one can take a negative attitude, saying that the PA is unable to guarantee security, or one can take a positive approach – which is the one the Commission is taking – which is that everything should be done to help them to be successful. We need to help them convince the Israelis that they can do this. And this is what this police project is about.

This project is part of a much larger support framework materialised by the mission EUPOL COPPS (EU Police Mission for the Palestinian Territories): the EU is increasing the staff of the Mission and making them re-engage with the local police. Don't forget that for the last two years we could not reach the police because of the situation created by the Hamas Government.

Now EUPOL COPPS really needs to show some progress quickly. So that's where the IfS comes in, because it can deliver assistance very quickly, contrary to complex development projects which are subject first to a dialogue and agreement with the Palestinians, then the preparation of documents which must be discussed with all stakeholders. It takes several months for a standard project to take off and implementation can then take several years. The IfS is something that can happen very rapidly. And this has a key importance because the PA cannot afford to wait three years to prove to the Israelis that they can manage security: they have to do it now. So security is the number one priority of the PA government of Prime Minister Fayyad. This comes together in the Berlin Conference in Support of Palestinian Civil Security and Rule of Law, which will provide international support to the PA in its efforts to develop an effective and reformed security sector.

Support for the Quartet

An EU mission to support the office of the Quartet Representative started operations in September 2007. The EU is the biggest donor among the four Quartet members: its specific activities to support the Office of the Quartet Representative in Jerusalem are financed through the IfS activities for Palestine launched in late 2007.

A Palestinian man from Gaza crosses the Erez checkpoint from Israel to Gaza, May 24, 2006.

© Alexandra Boulat / Agence VII / Palestine

The Second Intifada. Palestinians prepare to bury 30 countrymen killed by the Israeli Army in the Jenin refugee camp.
April 19, 2002. Israel launched controversial, large-scale military operations across the occupied Palestinian territory,
killing militants and civilians, following a spate of deadly Palestinian suicide bombings in Israel.
© Alexandra Boulat / Agence VII

The Second Intifada. Burial of 30 dead Palestinians killed by the Israeli army in Jenin refugee camp.
© Alexandra Boulat / Agence VII

Hamas Security Chief. Youssef Zahar. Hamas militia members pray in a mosque in Gaza City, May 26, 2006.
© Alexandra Boulat / Agence VII

The mandate of the Quartet Representative is to improve the economic situation, building activities and finding donor support. Its main objective is therefore to develop and create a momentum: an atmosphere conducive to positive developments, in the political process. Now the two-state solution has been accepted, but there are still so many drawbacks in the lives of Palestinians because of the situation on the ground. So Palestinians are now very sceptical that positive results can be achieved. But on the whole the assessment of the people is that this is worth another try. In this respect the conferences in Annapolis and Paris were very important. The meetings themselves, and the presence of Tony Blair as the Quartet's Special Representative, strengthened the impression that the international community is stepping up its activities to support the Palestinian Authority. They were instrumental in convincing donor countries and the international community that no results could be achieved without a change on the ground from Israel, that Palestinians would not be a threat and that the lives of the people would improve. It was important to prove to Palestinians and Israelis, but especially to Palestinians, that the situation is changing and that what we are asking from them will bring results. Our main aim is to deliver. So we tend to work on concrete projects that can bring positive results.

Solving issues on the ground

There was the case of a sewage lake in the north of the Gaza Strip, just above the village of Beit Lahia. It was filled with the untreated overflow from the local sewage plant. The plant had been struggling for a long time to recycle the waste. In March last year the dam of a separate smaller basin at the same site broke and the flooding killed five people. But if the main lake's embankment breaks it will be a disaster and many people will lose their lives. The World Bank has been working on this project through donors including the EU, trying to improve the situation, but it has been blocked for three years because of Israel's decision to impose curbs on the shipment of raw materials and goods into Gaza. One of the fears of Israel was that the metal pipes necessary to complete the work might be used to build rudimentary rocket-like weapons. The international community convinced the Israelis that the lake was also dangerous for Israel, that there was the risk of it contaminating the underground water that flowed into Israel. So the problem seems now on the way to a solution, and this is very important for the donors who will see concrete results, and for the PA who will be able to prove to the local people that they are doing a concrete project for them. There are other issues on which we are now working. High-level political meetings are scheduled in order to carry out new actions to secure the acceptance of key economic and security projects. But the finalisation of any project between Palestinians and Israelis is linked to the decisions that Israel will take relating to the movement of people. This is a very important question. We have to see what the concrete results on the ground will be.

Children looking for a class room in Beit Hanun after the Israeli Autumn Clouds military operation which left 65 people dead in a week time, North of Gaza, November 14. 2006.
© Alexandra Boulat / Agence VII

The Second Intifada. Jenin refugee camp after Israeli raid.
© Alexandra Boulat / Agence VII

A man herds sheep next to the separation wall between Israel and the occupied Palestinian territory in Bethlehem,
Palestine on March 19, 2007.
© Alexandra Boulat / Agence VII

SOMALIA

Support to the African Union AMISOM Planning Unit

REPORTAGE BY AMY SHIFFLETTE

PHOTOGRAPHS & CAPTIONS BY FRÉDÉRIC COURBET

Somali women in Eyl village.
© Frédéric Courbet / Agence VU / Somalia

© GOPA-Cartermill

Capital: Mogadishu

Area: 637,000 km²

Border countries: Djibouti 58 km, Ethiopia 1,600 km, Kenya 682 km

Population: 8,699,000 (2007)
Note: Estimate of UN World Population Prospects (2006 Revision) including Somaliland
Median age: 17.6 years
Life expectancy at birth: male 46.4 years; female 49.9 years (2005)

Government type: transitional regime with one legislative body

Note: "New transitional government" from October 2004 (with its legislature based in Baidoa from February 2006 through December 2007) lacked effective control at the end of 2007

GNI – per capita: US$ 274 (2006)

Source: © 2008 Encyclopædia Britannica, Inc.

A man drives through the streets of Eyl, Puntland in a vehicle named 'Technical'.
It is an all-terrain vehicle with a heavy weapon — a type of an anti-aerial canon (the photo is without the canon).
© Frédéric Courbet / Agence VU / Somalia

INTRODUCTION

Mohammed Siad Barre, the former despotic leader of Somalia, once said, 'When I came to Mogadishu ... [t]here was one road built by the Italians. If you try and force me to stand down, I will leave this city as I found it. I came to power by the gun; only the gun can make me go.'[1]

His proclamation is laden with 17 years of irony: Siad Barre's overthrow in 1991 and the transition that followed were marked by internal discord and violent insurgency between clan warlords. It was widely hoped that the end of his 20-year dictatorship would usher in peace and rule by consensus. Instead, conflict has beset the country ever since; all attempts to restore peace and governance have failed.

It is not just 'power by the gun' that characterises the situation in Somalia. Unrelenting famine, draught and disease have paralysed this country of mostly pastoralists. Even before the most recent major drought in 2006, Somalia had one of the highest malnutrition rates in the world. Currently, food and food aid are difficult to acquire, the latter frequently stolen by gun-wielding insurgents.

It is difficult to assess the real scope of the situation, as facts and statistics don't carry much validity in Somalia. The number of internally displaced persons (IDPs) ranges from 350,000 (United Nations Somalia) to 1,000,000 (Internal Displacement Monitoring Centre). During two weeks in November 2007 alone, an estimated 200,000 fled Mogadishu. The *CIA World Factbook* indicates a

(1) Mohamed Diriye Abdullahi (2001), *Culture and Customs of Somalia,* Greenwood Press, United States, p. 41.

1960	Italian Somaliland and British Somaliland unite to form the United Republic of Somalia
1964	Border dispute with Ethiopia erupts into violent clashes
1969	Muhammad Siad Barre assumes power in coup d'état
1988	Peace accord signed with Ethiopia, re-establishes diplomatic relations
1991	Siad Barre is ousted, igniting a power struggle between clan warlords. Thousands of civilians are killed or wounded. Former British protectorate of Somaliland declares independence
1993	US Army Rangers are killed when Somali militias shoot down two US helicopters in Mogadishu. A battle follows, killing hundreds of Somalis.
2000	Clan leaders and senior figures meet in Djibouti. The first government since 1991 is formed.
2001	Somali warlords, backed by Ethiopia, announce their intention to form a national government, in direct opposition to the country's transitional administration
2004	In the 14th attempt since 1991 to restore a central government, a new transitional parliament meets in Kenya
2006	February: The transitional parliament meets in Somalia for the first time March and May: Scores of people are killed during fierce fighting between rival militias in the worst violence in nearly a decade

September: Militias loyal to the ICU take control of Mogadishu and other parts of the south after defeating clan warlords

December: UN Security Resolution endorses African peace-keepers, specifying that neighbouring states should not deploy troops

28 December: A joint Ethiopian and Somali Government force captures Mogadishu

2007   February: UN Security Council authorises a six-month African Union Mission to Somalia, known as AMISOM. The mandate has since been extended to July 2008.

March: African Union peace-keepers land in Mogadishu amid battles between insurgents and TFG forces backed by Ethiopian troops. The Red Cross claims it is the worst fighting in 15 years.

July: National reconciliation conference opens in Mogadishu and comes under mortar attack. Refugee flight grows amid upsurge in violence.

2008   January: Nur Hassan Hussein, also known as Nur Adde, is sworn in as Prime Minister. The number of Somalie refugees reaches 1 million

population of 9,118,773 with a notable disclaimer: 'this estimate was derived from an official census taken in 1975 by the Somali Government; population counting in Somalia is complicated by the large number of nomads and by refugee movements in response to famine and clan warfare'. Somalia is not ranked in the 2007 UN Human Development Index because of its inability to provide data.

Recently the country has acquired a new distinction: in 2007 UN Secretary General Special Representative Ahmedou Ould-Abdallah pronounced Somalia's humanitarian crisis the worst in Africa.

The rise and fall of the Islamic Courts Union

After the collapse of the Siad Barre regime in 1991, a structure of Sharia-based Islamic courts became the principal judicial system. Over time these courts began to offer other services such as education, policing and healthcare. Initially they enjoyed wide public support. In 1999 the various courts began to assert their authority; supporters of the Islamic courts and other institutions formed the Islamic Courts Union (ICU), an armed militia. Until the end of 2006 the ICU controlled most of southern Somalia, including the capital, Mogadishu. The Islamic courts were credited with bringing unprecedented stability to a city plagued by lawlessness and extreme violence. It is widely reported that the ICU benefited from support of foreign governments, including neighbouring Eritrea.

In December 2006 Somalia's historic rival Ethiopia intervened in Somalia to oust the ICU in support of the country's transitional federal government (TFG). Ethiopian and TFG troops ousted the

A car body is stranded on the rocks next to the Haafun Village on the coast of Somalia. The tsunami aftermath on this part of the coast has displaced and damaged this car, as well as many houses.
© Frédéric Courbet / Agence VU / Somalia

PROJECTS FACTS & FIGURES

Programme
Strategic management, planning and monitoring of African Union (AU) peace support mission in Somalia (AMISOM)

Locations
African Union Headquarters in Addis Ababa, Ethiopia. Liaison team in Nairobi, Kenya.

Amount funded by the IfS
€5 million

Duration
18 months (until mid-2009)

Human resources deployed
33 planners in Addis Ababa, four planners in Nairobi. Additional support staff including secretaries, drivers and security guards.

Target groups/beneficiaries
African Union, AMISOM

ICU in a matter of days. Although the campaign was conducted in the name of fighting international terrorism, Ethiopia's actions were rooted in its own regional and national security interests: namely, a proxy war with Eritrea.

Since the establishment of Ethiopian and TFG troops in Mogadishu in January 2007, residents of the capital have regularly endured attacks by insurgent forces aimed at Ethiopian and TFG military forces and officials. In response, Ethiopian/TFG forces have launched mortars, rockets and artillery fire, often killing civilians.

In March 2007 Ethiopian forces launched their first offensive to capture Mogadishu's stadium and other locations, which met resistance from a widening coalition of insurgent groups. Hundreds of civilians died trying to flee or while trapped in their homes as the rockets and shells landed. Tens of thousands of people fled the city. On 26 April 2007 the TFG, which played a nominal role supporting the Ethiopian military campaign, declared victory. Within days insurgent attacks resumed, and violence has continued through to the present.

Signs of hope

A positive dynamic has recently entered into the Somali political process: namely, the nomination of Prime Minister Nur Adde on 10 January 2008 by an overwhelming majority (223 votes in his favour out of 230). His new government is considered to be comprised of highly regarded individuals from civil society with direct contacts with the opposition. Nur Adde has focused on dialogue with the opposition and shown openness to freeing imprisoned media representatives.

AMISOM AND THE EUROPEAN UNION'S RESPONSE

A stable Somalia is crucial. Conflict and its destabilising consequences affect the entire Horn of Africa region. The European Union recognises the importance of a secure Somalia, and directly engages through bilateral initiatives as well as in the context of the EU Strategy for Africa, the EU Strategy for the Horn of Africa and most recently the Instrument for Stability (IfS).

Achieving peace and stability in Somalia has been a priority particularly for the European Commission. The Commissioner for Humanitarian and Development Aid, Louis Michel, has been personally committed to driving this process forward. He visited Baidoa and Mogadishu on 20 December 2006, urging the ICU and the TFG to resume dialogue and avoid further conflict.

The Commission continues to work actively alongside the African Union. The AU Mission in Somalia (AMISOM) was deployed in March 2007 on the basis of UN Security Council Resolution 1744 to help stabilise Somalia and create a secure environment for reconciliation talks. The inherent difficulty of this mission is extraordinary, especially as only 1,600 Ugandan troops and 440 Burundian troops of a planned 8,000-strong mission have so far deployed.

The 30 January 2008 communiqué of the International Contact Group (ICG) on Somalia emphasised the importance of security and stability in the humanitarian and political situation. 'The ICG calls on troop contributing countries to expedite the deployment of additional troop contributions …. The full and timely deployment of AMISOM and the strengthening of Somali security institutions will help create the conditions for Ethiopia's withdrawal from Somalia.'

INSTRUMENT FOR STABILITY AMISOM PLANNING UNIT

The IfS programme in Somalia funds a specific aspect of the overall AMISOM mission: the establishment and functioning of the AMISOM PU. This unit is based within the AU Commission Headquarters in Addis Ababa, Ethiopia, and includes a small liaison team in Nairobi, Kenya.

The programme, which will last 18 months, will fund the salaries of a full team of 33 African planners and crisis response experts recruited by the African Union, as well as related functioning costs of the Plannng Unit including a team of four planners/experts in the Nairobi liaison office. The PU is comprised of four groups: operations, civil action planning, police planning and military planning. It is entrusted with the strategic management, planning and monitoring of the ongoing AMISOM mission.

The IfS programme aims to strengthen the AU Peace and Security Department's strategic management, planning and operational capacity in relation to AMISOM. A further objective is to provide the needed strategic planning, management and guidance to AMISOM, reducing the dependence on ad-hoc, short-term appointments of planners and experts. The programme equally aims to strengthen African conflict prevention, management and resolution capacities.

Although the IfS programme will operate until mid-2009, the Planning Unit is set to become a lasting AU structure. It is foreseen that the Tenth European Development Fund (EDF) through the Africa Peace Facility (APF) capacity-building programme will take over the running costs of the PU, which should provide funding for an additional three years.

PROJECT OBJECTIVES

To support the establishment and functioning of the AMISOM Planning Unit (PU). To reinforce the effectiveness of the ongoing substantive EU support to AMISOM and the strengthening of the African conflict prevention, management and resolution capacities.

Specific objective:
Endowing the AU Commission with a genuine capacity to provide the requisite strategic planning, management and guidance to AMISOM.

Expected results:
With a functional management and planning capacity within the context of AMISOM, the PU is set to become a lasting AU structure.

INTERVIEW | **MICHELE CERVONE D'URSO**
Somalia Desk Officer, EC Directorate-General
for Development

The European Union has consistently sought a political solution to the Somali crisis. In late December 2006, I accompanied European Commissioner for Development and Humanitarian Aid, Louis Michel, to Mogadishu and Baidoa, Somalia. This was a peace mission to clinch a possible agreement between the Transitional Federal Government and the Islamic Courts Union just before conflict erupted between the ICU and the TFG and Ethiopian forces.

By the end of 2006, Ethiopian troops entered the Somali capital, Mogadishu, for the first time. The ICU, which had controlled southern Somalia, was routed. Since January 2007 there has been growing insurgency in Mogadishu and southern Somalia. So far, the military strategy to pacify southern Somalia has not succeeded and many of the rifts between the TFG and Islamic courts still prevail.

This has had significant implications on the geostrategic configuration of the Horn of Africa. It is important to keep in mind the broad implications of the Somali conflict: Ethiopia and Eritrea are fighting a proxy war in Somalia. Together with the Middle East, the region is one of the most conflict-prone regions in the world. AMISOM has a critical role in the disengagement of these two countries, and the challenges the international community has placed on the African Union are enormous.

It is now time for the European Union to re-engage with the Somalian crisis. It is not something far away: if one looks at trafficking, refugees, terrorism, fragile state considerations, it can truly affect Europeans on a daily basis. The Somalis have been suffering for more than a decade and a half:

A tank abandoned next to the airport of Bossasso, Somaliland [breakaway territory of Somalia].
© Frédéric Courbet / Agence VU / Somalia

A young Somali woman in the Eyl village.
© Frédéric Courbet / Agence VU / Somalia

we're talking about 1.5 million displaced persons in the past few months.

We must respond. The Somalis are very resilient people – they're pastoralists – and they've gone through everything. At a certain point their coping mechanisms might not be able to sustain it and we could have a major humanitarian disaster. Somalia could potentially have a dramatic impact, as far as refugees going to Kenya, Yemen, Saudi Arabia and to Europe.

We are confident that the different parties realise they cannot win through conflict. There could be an opportunity to push forward the political process if they are willing to sit around the negotiation table. The international community has been calling for a transitional government which is open to engage with all political forces. The nomination of a new government under the leadership of Prime Minister Nur Adde provides renewed hope to re-launch the transitional and reconciliation processes.

It is important that the international community help create conditions for all the Somalis –including the opposition – to be engaged in the transitional process: a constitution, census, political parties and elections. This is the political game from now until 2009. In this context AMISOM has a key role in ensuring security, if not directly at least in monitoring a possible ceasefire process. At the moment we are in a very complex situation because we have a peace-keeping operation in a fully fledged conflict situation.

A car body stranded in the Haafun village on the Somali coast. The tsunami aftermath on this part of the coast has displaced and damaged this car as well as many houses.
© Frédéric Courbet / Agence VU / Somalia

A young man walking in the Haafun village on the Somali coast. Hit by the tsunami, the Haafun community struggles to survive along the coast line, fishing sharks and lobsters to be sold to the rest of the world in an 'uncontrolled way'. Maritime authorities continuously warn about the dangers of Somali waters but since the country remains divided between fiefdoms controlled by rival warlords, there is no single authority that can control the 3,300 km long coastline. Ships that continue to sail close to the coast in order to trade commercial goods and deliver humanitarian aid are frequently attacked by pirates. The 'Pirates' are usually Somalis trying to make a living from what they can find.

© Frédéric Courbet / Agence VU / Somalia

Road to reconciliation

The main actors involved, apart from AMISOM and the TFG, are the Ethiopians and the insurgents. The insurgents are divided between the Alliance for Reliberation of Somalia, the extreme Islamic youth movement – the shebabs – and clan-based militias. The European Commission, Italy, Norway, Sweden, the United Kingdom and the United States are the main donors, which also comprise the International Contact Group for Somalia. This body coordinates international policy in Somalia under the leadership of the UN Special Representative of the Secretary General (UNSRSG).

In this political context, the UN Security Council (UNSC Resolution 1744) authorised on 20 February 2007 the deployment of AMISOM, to accompany the political and reconciliation processes, enhance security and create the conditions which would allow for Ethiopian withdrawal. This process has been backed by the European Union and its General Affairs and External Relations Council (GAERC), which reconfirmed on 10 December 2007 that the European Union should support the enhancement of AMISOM.

AMISOM deployed in March 2007. There are approximately 1,600 Ugandan troops and more than 400 Burundian troops now in Mogadishu. They control the seaport, the airport and the residence of the president (Villa Somalia). Of course, this contingent does not suffice to pacify Somalia; they can hardly manage to take care of their own security. ,

The challenges AMISOM faces are enormous, the first of which is ensuring it is linked to the larger political process. They should basically support the political and ceasefire processes, and they're ill-equipped to do either. We are therefore encouraging AMISOM to play a facilitating and monitoring role.

A young Somali woman draws water in the village of Haafun. The aftermath of the tsunami on this part of the coast left the wells polluted by the sea water.
© Frédéric Courbet / Agence VU / Somalia

Two young women in the streets of Bossasso, one of them using her mobile phone.
© Frédéric Courbet / Agence VU / Somalia

Another challenge is that we cannot run a peace operation only with Ugandan and Burundian troops. More resources are needed. In the mandate approved by the UN Security Council and the AU Peace and Security Council, 8,000 troops were expected in Somalia. The international community continues to encourage other contributor countries such as Nigeria and Ghana to deploy as soon as possible to Mogadishu. The fact remains that potential troop-contributing countries are concerned about the intensity of the conflict. As a result, they're not deploying. They are concerned about the safety of their troops, that there is no political process and that there are not enough financial resources on the table.

A young Somali woman standing in front of her house in the city of Garowe.
© Frédéric Courbet / Agence VU / Somalia

Innovative funding

One of the main lessons learned from the African Union Mission in Sudan (AMIS) operation in Darfur is the need for strategic management and planning of a peace-keeping operation by the African Union. It is here where European Commission support to AMISOM via the IfS comes in. We provide €5 million for the establishment of an AMISOM Planning Unit. In addition to the resources from the IfS, the European Commission provides a contribution of €15 million from the African Peace Facility to cover the running costs of AMISOM. I think AMISOM is one of the most innovative support mechanisms under the IfS. It is the only one in the world where we directly support a peace-keeping operation.

The contribution from the IfS can have a major impact in bringing stability to Mogadishu. It can also help foster the political process and the dialogue between the traditional federal institutions and the opposition.

The IfS will ensure that 28 planners manage and plan the operation from the AU headquarters in Addis Ababa. It will also enhance the AU team in Nairobi, enabling the AU to focus on the linkages between the peace-keeping operation and the security sector reform aspects. These are mainly supported through bilateral funding such as the EC-funded Rule of Law and Security programme (ROLS). The Commission is contributing €10 million for the ROLS programme, which supports police training and stabilisation in Mogadishu.

Though the IfS contribution doesn't directly support peace-keepers, as this is done through the APF, it supports the civil, planning part of the operation. This civilian wing is made up of detached military personnel of the Member States. While the strategic management of the operation will be from Addis Ababa the operational management is from Mogadishu and funded by the APF. It's very important that the AU sets up its headquarters in Mogadishu as soon as possible so that the daily management of the operation can be more effective.

Planning for peace

I think we have been able to respond fairly swiftly. The IfS contribution was identified by the Commission in March 2007. We had two follow-up missions in July and August, and the Commission took a decision in October 2007. We are working very closely with other partners such as Italy, Sweden and the United Kingdom, as well as the United States. The United Kingdom had been funding some of the planners, so we are taking over an initiative from a Member State but expanding it further. We signed an agreement which took effect on 1 December 2007 and will run for 18 months. We are also encouraging more structured support and the potential takeover of the operation from the United Nations. We should not treat Somalia differently from any other country.

The AMISOM Planning Unit is comprised exclusively of Africans, mainly military personnel from AU member states as well as local staff recruited in Addis Ababa. Our resources are channelled directly to the African Union. We follow their recruitment, financial and contractual procedures. This venture is very much in the hands of the African Union, which underlines the partnership the European Union has with the African Union. A new EU Delegation to the African Union has opened, which will specifically be responsible for managing this programme in close coordination with the EC Special Envoy for Somalia and his team, who are based in Nairobi.

Ultimately our objective is to promote through AMISOM an inclusive political process in Somalia and double-track political and security strategy. The alternative of pursuing a military strategy alone could polarise further the region and give undo credence to extremists. To some extent it is also about helping the transitional institutions to win hearts and minds of the population. The European Commission remains committed to support relentlessly the Somali people and an inclusive political process.

An AK 47 assault rifle is lying on the seat of an all-terrain vehicle named 'Technical'.
In Somalia one can buy a rifle like this without a licence at a price of US$ 300.
© Frédéric Courbet / Agence VU / Somalia

A man from the local militia patrolling, under the orders of the police of Puntland, the village of Haafun, on the Somali coast.

© Frédéric Courbet / Agence VU / Somalia

| JEREMY BRICKHILL,
| EC security adviser

As a security adviser, my starting point has been that a military option in Somalia has never been viable. So far the indications are that I am right. The Ethiopian armed intervention, has succeeded in provoking and mobilising large numbers of angry young people who want to fight the occupiers.

The European Commission is still hoping for a good ending to this débâcle, but I think it's actually pretty bleak. There are literally hundreds of young people joining the shebab movement, and they will continue to win public support so long as they are seen as fighting a foreign occupation. What was a policy option to reduce radicalisation has essentially worked the other way around

There is fighting all over Mogadishu today. Whether this is a full-fledged offensive or just a dress rehearsal for more conflict is not yet clear. But on the whole I think the numbers are on the side of the insurgency. There is really limited political space for opposition, so the opposition are turning to the insurgency as the only way to express their frustration about the Ethiopian armed intervention. They have recruited very successfully over the past eight or so months and have trained large numbers of people. Meanwhile, massive numbers of arms are flowing in; there is no shortage of arms and ammunition. Then there is the massive amount of public support, and with more than 600,000 displaced people you can imagine which way public support goes. I think we're getting close to the endgame – it's just a question of how this plays out.

I can compare this experience with the situation in Sudan and the Comprehensive Peace Agreement where I worked as adviser on the security arrangements during the negotiations. The key difference there was that there was strong donor coherence, and in the case of Somalia we simply don't have that.

There is very little ground now on which to move. From a Somali perspective the United Nations has been characterised by its deafening silence in the face of continuous and very obvious human rights abuses by all parties. In that regard, the Commission and one or two Member States have been able to keep more neutral, and I hope that is going to enable us to play a more positive role. Without a substantive policy change the likelihood is that you're going to have a much more radicalised Islamic government in Mogadishu within a matter of months.

Gathering momentum

With regard to the establishment of the AMISOM peace support operation, I think the mandate was poorly thought through politically, which made the mission suspect in the eyes of Somalis. This has been the first case where a peace-keeping operation doesn't have a civilian protection mandate since the Rwandan genocide, and the Somali resistance has not been slow to argue that AMISOM simply stood aside watching as the Mogadishu civilian population were shelled by artillery and then systematically driven from the capital.

Despite the poorly drafted mandate I think the Ugandans have successfully negotiated themselves a broadly acceptable and low-profile presence and avoided getting dragged into the widening conflict. My advice in that regard has been for them to keep a low profile and maintain some kind of presence: in other words, keep them out of the

A young Somali woman comes out of her provisionally built shelter.
Her house, on the Somali coast in the Haafun area, was destroyed by the tsunami.
© Frédéric Courbet / Agence VU / Somalia

conflict until an opportunity for a ceasefire arose. We have been trying to get the Commission to push the ceasefires and try to get some momentum behind them. This has been difficult in a situation where there have been no red lines and little political will to push for a ceasefire. Nevertheless, there are opportunities for that even if they're localised; I have been pushing not for main ceasefires between big belligerents but even trying to find local disengagement humanitarian ceasefires as ways to get in.

One could look at AMISOM as having various functions which have not been addressed in the mandate, for example to verify and monitor ceasefires, help in military mediation, and provide effective support to a peace process, reconciliation and negotiations. In this regard extension of the numbers of forces on the ground is only one consideration. Perhaps more important might be to identify and support the specialist capacities which AMISOM would need to fulfil these functions – ceasefire verification teams, military mediators and capacity to support joint security mechanisms, for example.

'A positive approach in a difficult situation'

In light of this and in the face of the circumstances which AMISOM faced, one of the useful things at the beginning of the AMISOM deployment was to look at how we could use Commission funding and add value in a more strategic way. First we looked at the experience of AMIS in Darfur and the weaknesses of the mission there, which in many respects are quite similar.

From here the IfS funding for the AMISOM Planning Unit was developed. It was an attempt to give the African Union support to develop a more strategic planning capability, including coordination with other international support such as through the UNDP Rule of Law Programme in Somalia. I think this was a positive approach in a difficult situation: we have resources onstream now into giving the African Union the capability to think through and plan for several of the problems I've just mentioned. Funding for the Planning Unit is something less conventional than a peace operation that only puts boots on the ground.

The AMISOM Planning Unit is also trying to link up the regional elements of this problem. In that regard, important lessons are being learned. First of all, we have an innovative approach and the IfS provides the basis to be innovative, to try to respond to much more specific complexities, and not to just dump money in the most immediately obvious place. I think this is an important illustration and indication of the thinking behind the IfS.

From our side we've seen that as flexible as IfS funding is, we still need to look at ways in which we can make it more innovative; for example, the ability to operate with multiple contractors or include specific skills that are maybe only available outside the African Union. Right now we want to recruit some retired African service chiefs and African specialists operating outside of the African Union and the AU member states, but the procedures and

Two armed men from the local militia are looking towards the horizon in the light of the sunset, in Haafun, on the coast of Somalia.
© Frédéric Courbet / Agence VU / Somalia

A young Somali woman comes out of her provisionally built shelter.
Her house, on the Somali coast in the Haafun area, was destroyed by the tsunami.
© Frédéric Courbet / Agence VU / Somalia

rules for that are not yet there. I think there has already been an important learning curve, and something useful would be to assess the IfS and see how well it works in the different countries where it is trying to address problems and conflicts. Already we can see that it has enabled us to respond in a way that is much more strategic than in the past.

Drawing from experience on the ground

The AMISOM Planning Unit can only function in an advisory capacity, so having things being accepted politically is out of our reach. We must work from within a policy construction that major players determine and give the best possible advice in the context with which we are presented.

I think however the IfS in the form of the Planning Unit is one of the interesting areas for the European Union. I noticed in the AU-EU Summit and other partnership documents and consultations that these issues of strategic thinking are currently being grappled with. We need to learn from the rather conventional, formal development assistance processes and structures of the past and apply them to the much more complex realities on the ground. I think that's where IfS funding and this particular experience is quite illustrative. Traditionally funding was for, as in the case of the Darfur AMIS mission, supporting a field headquarters, the various components of putting a peace-keeping force on the ground, financial support to the troop-contributing countries, equipment and the normal requirements of a military operation. What was missing were the kinds of things we have tried to address in the AMISOM Planning Unit using the experiences of Darfur and other operations.

In the context of this mission, we had existing investments in Somalia which had been run by international non-governmental organisations (NGOs) and the United Nations for many years. Many of these involved the security sector, such as police training, support for previous disarmament, demobilisation and reintegration (DDR) efforts, support for human rights and civil society. Then along came a peace support operation like AMISOM and the process started again from scratch. The Commission and the Member States participate in and fund both of these streams of support, but they are not coordinated or linked through a common strategy. One of the things I think will be achieved is having a more strategic view in which we try to coordinate the investments running through different strands. An investment through the United Nations would historically need to be coordinated with the investment in AMISOM so that it could draw on the experience on the ground, complement ongoing efforts and ensure there is not duplication or contradictory efforts.

In view of this, the first task we set for ourselves was to help the African Union move into a more coordinated framework with the other international partners so that AMISOM was not an afterthought but was integrated into existing activities and assets. Secondly, we were looking to assist the African Union in having a better information analysis capability – in other words, being able to plug into existing networks. The United Nations and all sorts of international NGOs and other networks have been there for years. We were trying to give the AMISOM commanders and AU leadership a better comprehensive analysis of the situation on the ground by putting funding into an instrument they wouldn't normally consider. Generally it would be a normal military operation with a commander, a chief of staff and somebody in charge of logistics.

A strategic investment

We are trying to invest in a way that will enhance the strategic capabilities of AMISOM. This is done through coordination, information and analysis, knowledge and linkages with existing networks, and trying to give the African Union a more strategic capability than simply footsoldiers and commanders on the ground.

An armed Somali man from the local militia is, under the orders of the police of Puntland, patrolling the Haafun village, on the Somali coast.
© Frédéric Courbet / Agence VU / Somalia

An armed man from the local militia is walking in front of a boat bringing fishermen off the Haafun coast in Somalia.
© Frédéric Courbet / Agence VU / Somalia

Through many years of these peace-keeping operations we have learned there is a big need to be more strategic, more innovative and more political about the process in the sense of understanding the complexities of conflict in a nuanced way. You really have to invest in this for a mission to place itself effectively.

There are many lessons still left to be learned, and we will learn from this and see how the SMPU works. What funding like the IfS really does, we hope, is help institutions grapple with difficulties for all parties in the partnership.

Of course, the AMISOM Planning Unit is a technical measure and will not resolve the question of whether the policy is correct or not. Its intention was to be a strategic investment. We might have decided to use the money for another 1,000 troops, but we wanted to not only help the African Union be more strategic in this mission, but also help the Peace and Security Commission develop medium and longer-term capabilities to address conflict in Africa. This means helping them deal with institutional reform and creating a unit that will help them continue to be more strategic.

This would even include being able to give better briefings to the political leadership in the African Union because they now have the capabilities to do that. All of these were definitely lessons learned out of the AMIS deployment, which was a typical conventional deployment initially but had several weak points. For Somalia, we tried to recognise these gaps at the outset and look at the IfS funding as a package that would help address those gaps and wouldn't have to deal with them piecemeal but with in-kind technical assistance. This is a piece of funding that could give the African Union the capability to address those sorts of problems we encountered in Darfur.

It is very important in terms of learning from previous mistakes, being more innovative and trying to address problems more effectively. That doesn't necessarily mean that this will bring peace to Somalia in the immediate future. In terms of our impact, in particular trying to help our partners to have better assets and capabilities, I'm optimistic that it will be an important instrument.

A Somali woman standing in front of the hospital entrance in Eyl, Somalia.
© Frédéric Courbet / Agence VU / Somalia

SYRIA

Support to Syrian basic education in areas affected
by a large influx of Iraqi refugees

REPORTAGE BY PATRICIA MCCRACKEN

PHOTOGRAPHS & CAPTIONS BY PAOLO VERZONE/AGENCE VU

School for Iraqi refugees children in Babila, a small dusty neighbourhood, 10km south of Damascus.
© Paolo Verzone / Agence VU

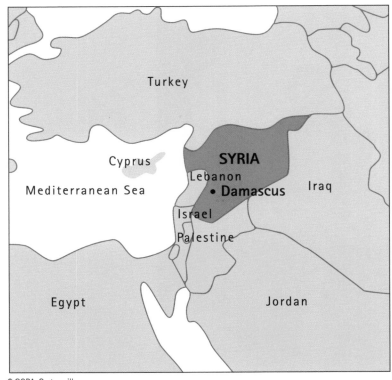

© GOPA-Cartermill

Capital: Damascus
Area: 185,180 km²
Population: 19,048,000 (2007)
Note: Excludes 1,400,000 recent Iraqi refugees and 450,000 longstanding Palestinian refugees in mid-2007

Life expectancy at birth: male 69.0 years; female 71.7 years (2006)
Government type: unitary multiparty republic with one legislative house
Source: © 2008 Encyclopædia Britannica, Inc.

Iraqi family waiting at the bus station in Sayeda Zeinab neighbourhood on the outskirts of Damascus that is home to many Iraqi refugees.
© Paolo Verzone / Agence VU

INTRODUCTION

Snaking through the desert sand is a line that traverses some 600 km, marking where Iraq ends and Syria begins. It is a place where dust devils descend, the wind whipping the sand into a frenzy, sending it storming like a mad army across the dunes. It is a harsh and hostile desert, and on the Iraq side, an unwitting host to a harsh and hostile war carried out by storms of men.

Since the start of the war, nearly 1.4 million Iraqis have journeyed over that line in the sand to Syria, running from the perils and tears that have marred and scarred their nation, and running to a country which has sworn to receive them always as brothers on native soil.

Syria made a constitutional vow in 1973 to be a nation for all Arabs, the 'beating heart of Arabism', where Arabs from other countries were granted a bill of rights within Syria's borders. The first of these rights was the elimination of entry visas: not only a symbolic gesture, but an implied invitation to stay. Other rights were more significant, and set down on paper every Arab's right to own property in Syria, to be provided with healthcare and social services courtesy of the state, and the right to a free education.

It is a diverse country, where Arabic and Aramaic tumble from the tongue; where Armenian, Kurdish and Circassian sounds spill from the shops and cafés; and even a dash of English is peppered into the joshing that goes on between men as they greet one another on the streets and in the squares.

Sayeda Zeinab neighbourhood on the outskirts of Damascus that is home to many Iraqi refugees.
© Paolo Verzone / Agence VU

In a spirit of brotherhood, this nation of 19 million has been merciful to its neighbours, having collected the citizens of the countries in collapse around it, keeping them safe, warm and fed. Syria has taken in some 500,000 Palestinians, around 50,000 Lebanese during the 2006 crisis, and the most consuming and trying number of all: an estimated 1.4 million Iraqis.

The first waves of Iraqis to cross into Syria were generally middle class, not as rich as their countryfolk who fled to Jordan. They brought with them their possessions, their savings and their job skills, albeit there were no jobs to be had, and the constitutional law does not extend to working rights.

With an average per capita yearly income of about US$ 4,000, Syria is considered, in World Bank speak, an MIC: a middle-income country. This means that non-government organisations (NGOs) and other aid groups set up there are often overlooked by donors in favour of countries which demonstrate more need. But with an economy already under duress because of US-imposed sanctions, Syria has been slipping further into crisis by absorbing so many Iraqis for such a sustained period of time.

In front the Sayeda Zeinab mosque, The Shrine of Sayidda Zeinab is a Iranian-style mosque and shrine in southern Damascus,.
It attracts Shia Muslim pilgrims from Iran and around the world.

PROJECT FACTS & FIGURES

Programme
Support to Syrian basic education in
areas affected by a large influx
of refugees from Iraq

Location
Damascus, Syria

Total amount sponsored by IfS
€3,000,000

Project start

Duration
18 months

Partners
European Commission, UNICEF
and Syria's Ministry of Education

Target groups
Schools with 50 or more Iraqi students.
These are in the neighbourhoods of
Damascus and rural Damascus which
have been affected by a large influx of
Iraqi refugees.

THE INSTRUMENT FOR STABILITY AT WORK
IN SYRIA: A LOOK AT THE PLAN

They've been called a 'ghost population', this exodus of Iraqis streaming out of their embattled homeland into Syria. They are not set up in tent cities at the border, with aid groups bringing in food supplies. They've moved into the cities and suburbs, mostly in and around Damascus, renting houses and apartments, driving cars, buying foods from local markets.

But the earlier arrivals have begun to run through their savings, and later waves have arrived with little or no savings to speak of. Some have begun to run illegal businesses as a means to support their families, and others are at risk of human trafficking.

They are an invisible populace that has swollen Damascus, pushing rents and prices higher, jamming the streets with ever more cars and the pollution they bring, straining the already overburdened local municipalities and public services.

But it is the Iraqi children who run in the shadow, their story untold, the facts of their young lives a foreboding of Syria's fragile future.

It's hard to know exactly how many Iraqi children are now living in Syria, but Syrian schools are struggling to cope with their numbers and their needs.

The schools in Damascus are deluged with students. Class sizes have doubled to about 50, there is a dire scarcity of books, desks, chalk, markers, electricity and working toilets, and teachers are bereft of skills to help young Iraqis who suffer from devastation and emotional scar tissue from the war they fled with their families.

Something had to be done, and the Commission shifted from analysis to action, drawing up an IfS project that outlined a concrete plan to ease the burden on the Syrian schools and come to the aid of the Iraqi children. UNICEF is the implementing partner of the IfS Project. The goals laid out were clear: increase the enrolment of Iraqi children; improve the structural conditions; train at least half of all teachers in basic psychosocial issues so they can better tend to the welfare of the more vulnerable Iraqi children.

At a UN conference in Geneva late in 2007 a cooperative venture between the European Commission, the Syrian Ministry of Education and UNICEF set up an 18-month programme, funded through the IFS.

Street scene in the Sayeda Zeinab neighbourhood on the outskirts
of Damascus that is home to many Iraqi refugees.
© Paolo Verzone / Agence VU

PROJECT OBJECTIVES

To improve the structural conditions of schools in Damascus; train at least half of all teachers in basic psychosocial issues so they can better tend to the welfare of the more vulnerable Iraqi children.

Background:
With class sizes doubled where there are large numbers of Iraqi students, the Syrian Schools infrastructure cannot handle the added numbers. Furthermore, only about 40,000 Iraqi minors in Syria are currently are enrolled in school. Yet it is believed there are about 300,000 school-age children now in the country. Thus, a campaign is under way to increase enrolment by 100 per cent.

Specific objectives:
- Buildings will be upgraded: fix broken windows, repair heating systems, repair toilets and water pipes, etc.

- More resources will be purchased, such as textbooks, desks, whiteboards and fans.

- Improved child welfare.

- Improved training of teachers, with at least 50 per cent of teachers specially trained to aid Iraqi children suffering from psychosocial disorders as a result of war. Teachers will also receive career training on active learning and school management techniques.

- Cultural, recreational and sports activities will be set up to provide students a structured environment to interact with each other.

193

Iraqi waiting at the bus station in Sayeda Zeinab neighbourhood
on the outskirts of Damascus that is home to many Iraqi refugees.
© Paolo Verzone / Agence VU

Sayeda Zeinab neighbourhood on the outskirts
of Damascus that is home to many Iraqi refugees.
© Paolo Verzone / Agence VU

School for Iraqi refugees children in Babila, a small dusty neighbourhood, 10km south of Damascus.
© Paolo Verzone / Agence VU

INTERVIEW | **FLORENCE LIOU GINGUAY**
International Relations Officer for Syria,
EC Directorate-General for External Relations

A plea for help

Last spring (2007) the Syrian government made a request for foreign assistance because they had challenges dealing with the refugee crisis. In this region things are already difficult, so we took the request very seriously and we wanted very much to help the government to cope with the refugee influx from Iraq.

Syria maintains a very subtle balance between values and religions. The country has been very generous with regard to the refugees fleeing violence in Iraq. There is no equivalent hospitality of this magnitude. Syria kept its borders wide open to the Iraqis for four years and continues to do so. In addition, the refugees do not live in camps in Syria, but they circulate freely and have access to all Syrian public services (although they cannot work).

It therefore seemed natural to answer favourably — and as quickly as we could — when the authorities asked for help.

Putting the IfS into play

There is both a human and a strategic dimension behind our support. Syria is a relatively stable country in a very unstable region. Communities coexist peacefully in Syria. Through this IfS activity, we wanted to diminish the risk of importing sectarian strife from Iraq and destabilising the country and the region further. This is a real danger.

Assessing the situation

There is a debate about the figures: the Iraqi population now in Syria is a difficult number to pinpoint because they blend in, they rent houses and apartments instead of living in tents in refugee camps, and there has been no infrastructure in place to adequately calculate the number. But it is safe to say that, to give a conservative number, there are at least one million refugees now in Syria, and this is a huge amount because Syria is a rather poor country. This massive number of people coming from Iraq who also have strong identities — Sunnis, Shi'as and Christians — has been hard on Syria and there then becomes a certain risk of destabilisation.

The refugees have put a lot of pressure on public services. Even though a small number of people have returned to Iraq, most are still in Syria, which is a great strain on the country. The reality is, the refugees will probably stay for years in Syria. So we needed to improve the conditions of the people in Syria, better integrate the Iraqi refugees, and at the same time not destabilise the country. In this case, we decided that we should have longer-term action and also help the authorities with the most essential structural assistance.

A call to action: working with UNICEF

So we started by providing a humanitarian response. The UN High Commissioner for Refugees (UNHCR) organised a large conference in Geneva, wanting to draw attention to the poorest of the refugees. (In Syria refugees tend to be poorer than the ones in Jordan.)

Just after that conference, we put together a first package of humanitarian assistance to help the most vulnerable, but it was not sufficient. We wanted to identify something that could be implemented relatively quickly. Basically through the IfS — which is really flexible — we decided to contact UNICEF.

We asked in what way we could react quickly, taking into account our current ongoing involvement in the country. But in addition, we wanted to do something in the education sector. Until now, we had never been involved in basic education, so we didn't have the expertise in working with the Minister

Delivery of supply
(by UNICEF & European
Commission) in a Iraqi
female school in Babila,
a small dusty neighbou-
rhood, 10km south of
Damascus.
© Paolo Verzone /
Agence VU

of Education. Therefore, we thought the best thing would be to go through a UN agency who was already active locally. So we contacted UNICEF on the spot. It turned out that they were already preparing a project, so we decided to respond to such an appeal.

Addressing the issues

The Iraqis in Syria have free access to schools. Any Arab child has access to public schools. But the thing is, the enrolment rate is relatively low. The United Nations estimates that 300,000 Iraqi children are refugees in Syria. Most likely, there are only 40,000 enrolled in Syrian schools, so the gap between the number of Iraqi children and the number of Iraqi students enrolled is enormous. There are several reasons for this. Statistics from the Ministry of Education may be incomplete, and at the same time, some parents don't send their kids to school because they need the child to work. And even though schooling is free, some schools are rejecting children because they

are already very overcrowded. And then there is the issue of documents: some kids likely didn't come to Syria with the documents they needed to enrol, so there you have a bureaucratic or legal issue. Here again, we have difficulty in assessing the figures.

Overall, the approach to this project is quite comprehensive: to help the government increase the capacity of schools, to raise awareness and increase enrolment, and to equip teachers with the skills to provide basic psychosocial support, since some of these children and adolescents have lived through very difficult experiences. Teachers will receive specific training for this.

And an important feature of this project is that it will benefit Iraqi and Syrian children alike. There is a strong wish of the government not to create parallel structures, a healthy principle to avoid creating tensions between the populations. The project follows an all-inclusive approach. All children

will have better-equipped schools in the areas where the capacity to welcome children has become insufficient. But the project will also address some of the specific needs of the refugees. So it is worth emphasising that the programme aims at encouraging Iraqi families to send their children to Syrian schools.

We anticipate that a result of this project will be that children and their families will be able to lead more 'normal' lives. Hopefully, there will also be more awareness and experience in Syrian institutions about what needs to be done to deal with strong psychological traumas. That is something that is not very developed in the region.

Integrating Iraqis in Syria

What is most striking in Syria is the diversity of its society and the wealth of cultural heritage. This is what makes the richness of its people and probably explains their open-mindedness and willingness to interact with others.

The idea is really to make sure that these Iraqis can integrate more easily into the Syrian society, and this means integrating the children as well. Given that there are many refugees, the integration has gone relatively smoothly so far, taking into account that the presence of the Iraqis has definitely strained communities in Syria by overcrowding, increasing prices, and introducing cultural differences.

Duma registration centre
for Iraqi refugees, a UNICEF
staff member with Iraqi
children
© Paolo Verzone /Agence VU

School for Iraqi children in the
Jaramana district near Damascus
© Paolo Verzone / Agence VU

Director of a school for Iraqi refugees in the Jaramana neighbourhood
© Paolo Verzone / Agence VU

INTERVIEW | ANIS SALEM
| UNICEF Ambassador in Damascus

Knowing the setting in Syria is very important to understanding the needs of the children and the project goals. Generally speaking, the country has good results for children in the area of education, despite the fact that the level of per capita income is not very high. So we have here a model of perhaps the classic socialism of the 1960s and 1970s, where social services were relatively good, especially child enrolment in schools and gender balance in enrolment.

Part of our challenge is that Syria is classified by the World Bank as being an MIC, a country that does not need massive infusions of international assistance, but needs more quality intervention to help monitor systems and move toward emerging issues that relate to child protection, quality education, early childhood learning and development.

What UNICEF brings to the table

UNICEF has been in Syria many, many years, about 40 years. We know our way around the country, the ministries and so on. We have the good will and the confidence of our counterparts.

We also have the ability to collect information, analyse it and see trends and raise our voice on these trends. And one of the first things we did in this context was a survey together with UNHCR and the World Food Programme about the situation of Iraqi refugees in Syria. It was conducted in 2006 and then distributed and analysed. We looked at the problems facing the refugees, including the level of income (Iraqis are not legally allowed to work in Syria), the housing situation and so on.

From analysis to action

Now, from there, we came to a new phase toward the end of 2006. UNHCR had announced its first appeal for a large-scale operation addressed specifically to refugees, and invited us to the Geneva conference in April. The high commissioner visited the region and started talking about issues. And I think this was an important visit. We got very involved with the Iraqi refugees issue here but despite our efforts we still felt somewhat demoralised because of the lack of donor support. And then suddenly things changed when we understood that the EU was really committed to help.

Making the pitch to the Ministry of Education

We estimate that there are 1.4 million Iraqis in Syria. So of that, how many are children? It is a hard number to get at specifically, but we took a very large sample and made some assumptions about the size of the family, the age range of the kids and so on. On that basis we came to an estimated number of Iraqi children of between 250,000 and 300,000. These are children who should be enrolled in schools, and the actual number of children enrolled was somewhere around 40,000.

Another aspect to consider in addition to funds was to get permission for the Instrument for Stability Project from the Syrian government. We began looking ahead toward the beginning of the school year and seeking ways by which we could enrol more kids in school. We could advocate this to the Ministry of Education, and actually to the minister in particular. We could stress the importance of Syria embracing all of the Iraqi children. This includes a translation of the rights of these children to an education, based on Syria's own 'open door' policy.

We could stress that this was advantageous to Syria since children in school are children in safe places, not subject to harm and not causing harm. We could stress that improving the educational structure for Iraqi refugee children was a long-term investment by Syria to gain the goodwill of an entire generation.

These were our key advocacy sales pitches. We also tried to do two other things. We tried to expand the vision. We tried, together with the Commission Delegation in Damascus, to convince the Ministry of Education to run a campaign to encourage enrolment. We encouraged this 'software' component, which included training teachers, equipping them to be able to welcome Iraqi children better, and to recognise their learning difficulties in the face of all that the children had been through.

The situation they are all confronted with includes more than 50 children in each class, more than double the normal size. There is also a strong difference in cultures. For example, in Syria, women wear lipstick, everyone carries mobile phones and so on. So there was a definite need to engage headmasters, teachers and parents in some sort of dialogue. Now this was a hard sell because the minister currently had a reform plan wherein he wanted to improve the quality for Syrian children, including smaller class sizes and more class hours. What he did not want to hear was that his goal of creating smaller class sizes for Syrians, and lengthening their class schedule, was at odds with our proposal to create double shifts to accommodate more Iraqi students. He could see that because of the big influx of even more Iraqi students his plans would be threatened.

Sayeda Zeinab neighbourhood on the outskirts
of Damascus that is home to many Iraqi refugees.
© Paolo Verzone / Agence VU

School for Iraqi refugees children in Babila,
a small dusty neighbourhood, 10km south of Damascus.
© Paolo Verzone / Agence VU

Portrait of Syria president Bashar Al Assad in a Taxi.
© Paolo Verzone / Agence VU

Plans in place

We are working with the Ministry of Education to improve 'hardware'. A large expanse of territory in Damascus and the surrounding area, known as rural Damascus, are the areas most affected by the influx of refugees. The present facilities are extremely poor.

We have put together on the basis of the IfS funds a package of support for these schools: furniture, whiteboards, fans for the summer, some kinds of heaters, things that would make the school environment a little better and more capable of supporting the students. Doing this also provides a message to the community. We shall also upgrade the school libraries, and we are looking at the possibility of expanding outside of Damascus.

As for 'software', one area of concern is keeping children engaged and supporting children who are experiencing trouble as a direct result of their trauma from the war. To address these needs, we are giving young people safe play areas and also referring children in need to specialists. We have research which shows that of 7,000 children, about 400 will need some sort of specialised attention related to their trauma.

So the way we are packaging things is that we're introducing a school-based protection dimension. We've been training teachers on handling situations where children need protection. They will be trained to detect when a child has been abused, when a child is distressed, and also how they can refer this child for further treatment. A manual is being developed that has been tested and printed for wider use.

The Peace-building Partnership

From Early Warning to Early Action Conference, November 2007.
Official launch of the Peace-building Partnership.

From Early Warning to Early Action Conference, November 2007.
Official launch of the Peace-building Partnership.

- Constitutes the crisis-preparedness component of the Instrument for Stability (Art 4.3.).

- Budget (2007-2008)
  €15 million.

- Aim
  mobilise and consolidate civilian expertise for peace-building.

- Addressed at
  non-state actors; international organisations; Member State agencies.

- First Call for Proposals
  March 2008.

- Second Call for Proposals
  May 2008.

More information

https://webgate.ec.europa.eu/tariqa/PeaceBuilding

andrew.byrne@ec.europa.eu

INTRODUCTION

Every day the media provide us with examples of the way that violent conflicts can destroy or ruin people's lives and livelihoods. Besides the immediate humanitarian misery that they cause, violent conflicts thwart ongoing efforts to reduce poverty, and horribly destabilise the social fabric of a society that is usually required for it to grow.

Fundamental to the EU is its commitment under the Treaties to 'promote peace, security and progress in Europe and in the world.' It recognises that 'peace, security and stability as well as human rights, democracy and good governance, are essential elements for sustainable economic growth and poverty eradication.'

The Instrument for Stability not only aims to create effective responses to a crisis situation, but also seeks to help foster these stable conditions under which recovery can occur. This requires a capacity to address global and transregional threats to stability. It also needs to ensure that people, organisations and societies are prepared to confront potential crises and to nip them in the bud, or to create the right conditions for recovery after a conflict has been resolved.

Preparedness is at the heart of the Peace-building Partnership. It provides funding to develop capacities for early-warning, mediation and reconciliation, and to address emerging inter-community tensions. It is also designed to tackle post-conflict and post-disaster recovery, by forming a bridge between immediate humanitarian aid, and the longer-term assistance required for recovery. It does this by ensuring that civilian expertise for these peace-building activities is mobilised and prepared for action.

CIVILIAN INVOLVEMENT IN PEACE-BUILDING

Creating and fostering the right conditions under which peace can take root and grow, is by no minds simple task. It is easy to overlook the extremely complex dynamics that are all required to be in place for peace to develop. Modern media often dwell on the easy-to-portray aspects of violent conflict: the point at which it erupts, and the efforts made to broker and manage the peace. We are familiar with TV footage of men in suits and/or uniforms negotiating the end of hostilities, and with film of more men in uniforms being deployed to keep the peace, and often being expected to restore it if the country spirals back into conflict.

Some of the conditions and services required for stable development can only be provided by state authorities: justice, security, healthcare, education etc. Overall, EU assistance – particularly for fragile states – is aimed at strengthening these conditions. However, moving towards lasting and effective peace needs to involve all layers and the entire structure of a society. Efforts need to involve the right players from the civilian sector to foster peace and help it to flourish. These civilian sector groups are also the best-placed people to detect any new emerging tensions, and press an alarm bell in good time, so that they do not get to the stage where they break out into widespread civil or military violence.

Citizens' groups are more apt to gain the trust of the people who stand to benefit most from peace-building. They are usually not perceived as partisan, and often work behind the scenes, out of the glare of media attention. They can be the unsung heroes of conflict resolution, as they work tirelessly to build bridges between communities to avoid or repair damaging splits. Local citizens' groups have often built up long-lasting relationships with international NGOs, based on trust and common aims.

Their experience and expertise is desperately needed to make peace, and to make peace work.

THE PEACE-BUILDING PARTNERSHIP

The European Union's Peace-building Partnership, launched during the "From Early Warning to Early Action" Conference in November 2007, aims to mobilise this expertise and build on it, so as to be better prepared for crises and how to avoid them, and to help deal with recovery after conflicts or disasters.

The Peace-building Partnership forms part of the 'crisis preparedness' component of the EU's Instrument for Stability, and is focused on building capacity among organisations and non-state actors. This can bolster the already substantial role they can play in tackling tensions before they become crises, and in creating the right conditions for recovery once peace is restored or after a disaster strikes. The Partnership will build up a network of specialised NGOs with expertise in early warning, conflict prevention, peace-building, and recovery after a conflict or disaster, and engage in a dialogue with them on ways of addressing specific problems of conflict prevention and resolution. It will also strengthen ongoing or develop new cooperation with other major partners: the UN, other international or regional organisations, and relevant agencies in the Member States.

Presence in the field is vital for gathering timely and relevant information on potential and developing conflict. Non-state actors are often the best-placed and most experienced sources of information, analysis and expertise. This has long been recognised within the EU, and the Commission as well as Member States often tap into this wealth of knowledge in order to better understand a crisis situation, and in order to map out a response to it.

DEVELOPING CAPACITIES

However, many non-state actors lack the funding to invest in their longer-term development, which can limit their capacities and effectiveness. They need to be able to put time into developing good practice, staff training, evaluation, and providing input to policy debates. The Commission's aim through the Peace-building Partnership is therefore to invest in these capacities.

The Partnership's first Call for Proposals — launched in March 2008 — has asked for organisations to table projects setting out activities to build these capacities, both within individual organisations, and between organisations in the way they network and share experience. Three types of capacities in particular are singled out under the first Call:

- Measures to strengthen the operational capacity of NGOs specialised in addressing state fragility, conflict, emerging inter-community tensions and early recovery from crisis.
- Development of capacity for informal ('track II and III') mediation and conflict-sensitive development.
- Conflict early warning systems and field-based political analysis in fragile states.

Activities to strengthen operational capacities could for example be aimed at strengthening the links between organisations in the field, and those operating at international level, so that information (early-warning signals and analysis) can flow faster and more freely between them. It can also help locally-based organisations have more of a say in policy debates at the international level, and in the way international groups represent their interests

MAPPING OUT EXPERTISE

There are many organisations working in different aspects of the conflict prevention, crisis management and peace-building. The Peace-building Partnership aims to develop a clearer picture of all these organisations and their activities.

The Partnership has set up a web portal (https://webgate.ec.europa.eu/tariqa/PeaceBuilding), designed to allow organisations working in the areas of conflict prevention, crisis management and peace-building, to provide information to the Commission on their activities. The portal is operational on the Europa website. Initially, organisations are asked to register on the portal with information about their activities in these areas. The resulting directory of organisations will enable the Commission to identify organisations with expertise in a particular region or sector.

At a later stage the portal will be a source of information on the current and planned activities of the Partnership, including Calls for Proposals. It could also eventually provide a forum for organisations to upload materials on their activities, or for discussion on the sorts of topics included under the Partnership.

CONSULTATION

While the Commission has for some time recognised the expertise of NGOs, and the fact that they are ideally-placed to provide key information about the situation on the ground, it also acknowledges a tendency to date to utilise civil society organisations simply as implementers for pre-selected tasks. Andrew Byrne manages the Partnership within the Crisis Response and Peace building Unit in the Commission's External Relations Directorate-General. He explained that up to now NGOs might be asked to write a report on – say – tensions surrounding water rights in a particular country, or on

ways of re-building specific aspects of society after a conflict. While their expertise was valuable in this regard, in effect this was only being requested within areas that had been pre-determined by the Commission. Both inside the Commission and among NGOs, the feeling was that these organisations could – and should – play a wider role.

A key notion behind the Peace-building Partnership is therefore to allow civil society organisations (CSOs) to feed in their expertise further upstream – into policy-making – and to advise the Commission on the themes, regions, or methodologies that it should be focusing on. Small grants will be available to cover the costs of preparing papers, and of taking part in the round tables and disseminating the results. Round tables should address relevant issues, which – for the first year of the Partnership's operations – are expected to include mediation, natural resources and conflict, gender issues, early warning and the contribution of technologies to crisis response and preparedness. During the second year of the Partnership's operations, the list of topics is to be expanded to include all activities covered by the crisis response component of the Instrument for Stability. The Commission is also planning to organise meetings at which an enhanced dialogue with CSOs can take place on key ongoing themes.

THE WAY FORWARD

Future calls for proposals will continue to give priority to capacity-building and to providing NGOs with an opportunity to set out their views on policy and approaches in the area of peace-building.

A network of ten civil society organisations devoted to conflict prevention and peace-building is already operational, funded by a specific budget line under the EU's 2006 and 2007 budgets, prior to the adoption of the Instrument for Stability. This 'Initiative for Peace-Building' was launched in September

2007 and will run under the current funding until September 2010. The ten organisations pool their expertise and geographical coverage in six main areas: security; gender; democratisation and transitional justice; mediation and dialogue; regional cooperation on environment, economy and natural resource management; and capacity building and training.

The Commission is keen to integrate this way of working through dialogue and provision of advice within the Peace-building Partnership, and to build on the progress being made here. New funding for networking of organisations in the sector will be available as part of the second Call for Proposals. This will initially run in parallel to the Initiative for Peace-Building, and gradually activities in this area will be integrated.

AN NGO RESPONSE

Philippe Bartholmé, of EPLO (the Brussels-based European Peacebuilding Liaison Office) explained that his organisation was happy that there is an Instrument for Stability: it's something that is really needed, and it provides vital money for European NGOs in this area. The NGO sector had ambitious aims in the peace-building area: it had been proposing a genuine European Peace-Building Agency – a counterpart to the European Defence Agency – that could provide a comprehensive response in crisis situations, and maintain an ongoing input to policy development. Although not an agency, Bartholmé explained, the Peace-building Partnership takes some small steps in this direction.

However, he did feel that there had been little in-depth consultation with the NGO sector, though recognised that this was to a large extent due to the short time-frame. The decisions on the new instruments were adopted by the EU very late in 2006, which meant that the resulting strategy paper and the first Annual Action Programme had to be drawn up extremely quickly, limiting time for real consultation. This had also meant that the range of topics on which NGO input was sought had been narrowed down by the time the Annual Action Programme was adopted. This went against the idea that NGOs should be able to bring their ideas to the table.

EPLO was pleased that the EC had decided to allow for smaller grants than originally planned. The NGO sector has recognised that smaller organisations face problems absorbing large grants under the conditions and duration of the contracts. It is now understood that grants can start from €50,000. This also means that there is likely to be a greater number of projects selected, with a greater variety of topics covered.

It remains to be seen how the civil society sector will approach the Call. In Bartholmé's view capacities might be better built through direct cash injections for organisations, which can provide the resources and therefore time to strengthen an organisation's capacity to provide early warning, or to improve its own working structures and methodologies. Financing rules do not allow for this, however, and so a Call for Proposals – perhaps better suited to a project-based approach – is the vehicle under which the funding will be provided.

BUILDING PEACE THROUGH WORK WITH OTHER ORGANISATIONS

Other elements of the Peace-building Partnership aim to build on the way the EU works with international and regional organisations on early warning and early recovery from conflict and natural disasters.

It is a cornerstone of the EU's development policy that aid should be coordinated with other donors, and should dovetail with it. During early recovery from conflict or disaster, there is a clear need for political stability, so that conditions are right to allow the steps to be taken from immediate post-crisis response to longer-term development. This requires active assessment of the needs of a country or region. The problem is that in the past, different donors have been carrying out different needs assessments using different methods. This can lead to dispersal of effort and confusion: not what a country struggling out of crisis requires.

Discussions are underway between the EU and the World Bank and UN on developing existing methodologies for needs assessment after conflicts and disasters, and funding under the Peace-building partnership will take this further.

The step from immediate humanitarian aid to reconstruction and recovery is also the focus of initiatives by the UN to form an 'early recovery cluster', involving a wider range of specialised partners. The cluster has looked at capacities for early recovery after natural disasters and conflicts and has identified a number of weak areas that require attention. Besides shortcomings in assessment tools, these weaknesses include gaps in training and inadequate access to data and expertise, plus difficulties in securing fast and predictable funding for recovery planning. The Peace-building Partnership will also contribute to the work going on in this cluster.

Cooperation with regional bodies is also to be developed under the Peace-building Partnership. In the 2007 Annual Action Programme, there is funding to strengthen the African Union's early warning system for conflict prevention. This will have a strong technical focus: remote sensing and modelling services developed by the EU's Joint Research Centre are to be customised to meet the needs of the AU. A set of conflict indicators, and a range of early warning systems will also be developed. These are all to be built on a strong technology basis, including open source intelligence tools, media tracking systems, and information exchange tools. Training in their use and the way they will be applied for early warning systems is also part of the package. This contribution will complement the work being carried out by the Africa Peace Facility, another EU-funded initiative, in fostering peace and security in Africa.

TRAINING

In 2000-2001 the EU decided to invest in strengthening civilian capabilities to support moves towards stabilisation in countries emerging from a political crisis. This training was to cover five main areas: police, rule of law, civilian administration, civil protection and monitoring.

Since then, this initiative has grown into a range of courses delivered by organisations from almost all Member States, and some 1,400 experts have taken part. Most recently, it has also trained almost 100 experts who had been selected to take part in special fact-finding missions, as part of Crisis Response Teams.

The Instrument for Stability will continue to fund this focus on training. It will finance work on a European training standard (including in principle the transfer of training modules already developed to other international organisations, notably the African Union), further training for Crisis Response Team members, as well as training to develop police expertise in civilian missions.